GCSE Edexcel
Additional Science
Foundation Workbook

This book is for anyone doing **GCSE Edexcel Additional Science** at foundation level.
It covers everything you'll need for your year 11 exams.

It's full of **tricky questions**... each one designed to make you **sweat**
— because that's the only way you'll get any **better**.

There are questions to see **what facts** you know. There are questions
to see how well you can **apply those facts**. And there are questions
to see what you know about **how science works**.

It's also got some daft bits in to try and make the whole
experience at least vaguely entertaining for you.

What CGP is all about

Our sole aim here at CGP is to produce the highest
quality books — carefully written, immaculately presented
and dangerously close to being funny.

Then we work our socks off to get them
out to you — at the cheapest possible prices.

Contents

Published by CGP

Editors:
Luke Antieul, Rosie McCurrie, Helen Ronan, Jane Sawers, Camilla Simson, Karen Wells,
Sarah Williams, Dawn Wright.

Contributors:
Paddy Gannon, Dr Giles R Greenway, Dr Iona MJ Hamilton, Frederick Langridge,
Sidney Stringer Community School, Paul Warren.

ISBN: 978 1 84762 766 7

With thanks to Katherine Craig, Mark A Edwards, Chris Elliss, Julie Jackson, Hayley Thompson
and Jane Towle for the proofreading.

With thanks to Jan Greenway, Laura Jakubowski and Laura Stoney for the copyright research.

Every effort has been made to locate copyright holders and obtain permission to reproduce
sources. For those sources where it has been difficult to trace the originator of the work,
we would be grateful for information. If any copyright holder would like us to make an
amendment to the acknowledgements, please notify us and we will gladly update the book at
the next reprint. Thank you.

Groovy website: www.cgpbooks.co.uk

Printed by Elanders Ltd, Newcastle upon Tyne.
Jolly bits of clipart from CorelDRAW®
Based on the classic CGP style created by Richard Parsons.

Cells

Q1 Plant and animal cells have **similarities** and **differences**.
Complete each statement below by circling the correct words.

a) (Plant)/ Animal cells contain chloroplasts.

b) Plant cells have **vacuoles** /(cytoplasm) containing cell sap.

c) (Both plant and animal cells)/ Only plant cells / Only animal cells have cell membranes.

d) The (cytoplasm) / **nucleus** is the gel-like part of the cell, where most of the chemical reactions happen.

Q2 Draw lines to match up each **part** of a bacterium to its correct **description**.

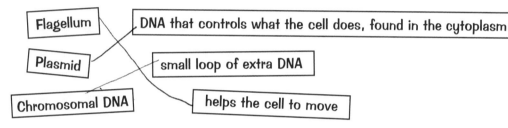

Flagellum	DNA that controls what the cell does, found in the cytoplasm
Plasmid	small loop of extra DNA
Chromosomal DNA	helps the cell to move

Q3 This question is about the **parts** of a cell.

Tick the boxes to show whether the following statements are **true** or **false**.

	True	False
a) The **nucleus** contains DNA.	✓	
b) **Chloroplasts** are where digestion occurs.		✓
c) The **cell membrane** gives support for the cell.	✓	
d) **Mitochondria** are where most of the reactions for respiration take place.	✓	

Q4 The diagram shows a typical **bacterium**.

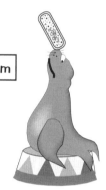

a) Name parts A, B and C on the diagram.

A chloroplasts

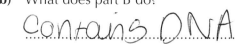

B Nucleus

C cell membrane

b) What does part B do?

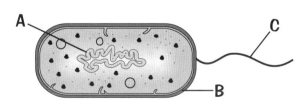

Contains DNA

Microscopes and DNA

Q1 **Microscopes** let us see things that we can't see with the naked eye.

A picture of a light microscope is shown below.

a) Complete the missing labels on the picture using the words listed below.

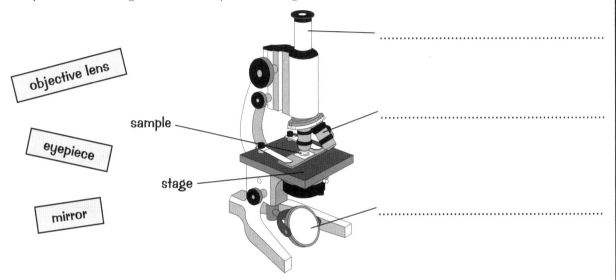

objective lens

eyepiece

mirror

sample

stage

b) Circle the parts of the microscope you would use to **focus** your image.

Q2 The following questions are about **DNA**.

a) What name is given to the shape of a DNA molecule? ....

b) How many different **bases** are there in DNA? ....

c) Draw lines to match the bases below with their correct base pair.

G   T

A   C

d) What type of bonds hold the base pairs together? ....

Q3 Professor Smart has invented a shrinking ray. He tests it on his cat, Fluffy, by shrinking him down to **0.06 mm long**.

The Professor looks at Fluffy using a **light microscope**. The image that he sees is **9 mm long**. Calculate the magnification of Professor Smart's image.

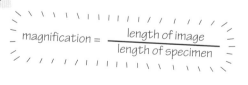

$$magnification = \frac{length\ of\ image}{length\ of\ specimen}$$

....

....

magnification = × ....

More on DNA

Q1 Complete the passage about the **discovery of DNA** using the words below.

| matched | Rosalind Franklin | x-rays | Francis Crick | pieces |

.... and Maurice Wilkins worked out that DNA had a helical (spiral)

structure. They found this out by firing beams of .... onto a crystal of

DNA and looking at the patterns this made. James Watson and ....

used these findings to make a model of DNA. From the studies of other scientists, they knew

that the amount of A + G .... the amount of T + C. They used all this

information to make a model of DNA where all the .... fitted together.

Q2 You can extract **DNA** from **onion cells** in a simple experiment in the lab.

a) The steps of this experiment are listed below.
Put them in the correct order by numbering the boxes. Some have been done for you.

5 Cool the mixture down again.

☐ Put the beaker in a water bath at 60 °C.

☐ Gently add some ice-cold alcohol.

1 Chop up some onion. Put it in a beaker with detergent, salt and water.

☐ Once ice-cold, put the mixture into a blender.

3 Put the beaker in ice to cool the mixture.

☐ Filter the mixture to get the froth and big bits of cell out.

☐ The DNA will appear as a stringy white substance. Fish it out with a glass rod.

b) Why is alcohol added to the mixture?

....

....

Top Tips: Your DNA controls what proteins your cells make — and they control everything the cells do. That's why the discovery of the structure of DNA was such a massive breakthrough in biology.

Genes and Proteins

Q1 Tick the boxes to show whether the following statements are **true** or **false**.

		True	False
a)	A gene is a section of DNA that contains the instructions to make a specific protein.	☐	☐
b)	Cells make proteins by putting amino acids together in a particular order.	☐	☐
c)	The order of bases in a gene tells the cells the order of the amino acids.	☐	☐
d)	Each type of protein gets made with a random number and sequence of amino acids.	☐	☐
e)	A protein's shape has no effect on its function.	☐	☐

Q2 Genes can have **mutations**. Put a tick in the box next to the statement that correctly describes what a mutation is.

☐ A change to all of an organism's genes.

☐ A change to an organism's DNA base sequence.

Q3 Complete the passage about **mutations** using the words below.

characteristics	protein	function	shape

A mutation could change the order of amino acids in a .... This could

change its ...., which could affect its ....

In turn, this could change the .... of an organism.

Q4 Draw lines to match each kind of **mutation** with what it means.

Harmful   A mutation that could produce a characteristic which is helpful.

Beneficial   A mutation that is not harmful or beneficial.

Neutral   A mutation that could cause a genetic disorder.

Enzymes

Q1   Complete the sentences below by circling the correct word(s) from each pair.

a)   An enzyme is a **biological catalyst** / **chemical reaction**.

b)   Enzymes **speed up** / **slow down** the useful chemical reactions in the body.

c)   A catalyst is a substance which **increases** / **decreases** the speed of a reaction without being changed or **copied** / **used up** in the reaction.

Q2   **Enzymes** are involved in all sorts of reactions in the body, both **inside** and **outside cells**.

Draw lines to match the **examples** of enzyme-catalysed reactions below with their **descriptions**.

DNA replication   Enzymes are released into the gut to digest food.

Protein synthesis   Enzymes hold amino acids in place and form bonds between them.

Digestion   Enzymes help copy a cell's DNA before it divides.

Q3   Chemical reactions usually mean things get split apart or joined together. The **substrate** is the molecule that is changed in a reaction.

a)   Enzymes are **highly specific** for their substrate. What does this mean?

   ....

b)   For an enzyme to work, the substrate must **fit exactly** into its active site. Give the name for this type of mechanism.

   ....

c)   The diagram below shows a chemical reaction involving an enzyme. Complete the diagram to show what happens to the substrate when the enzyme catalyses a reaction.

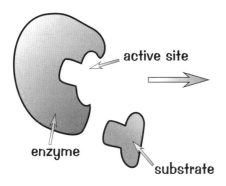

<u>*Enzyme Activity*</u>

Q1 You can investigate enzyme activity by looking at the action of enzymes and substrates. Complete the statements by circling the correct words from each highlighted pair.

a) Use amylase as the **enzyme** / **substrate**.

b) Use starch as the **enzyme** / **substrate**.

c) Amylase breaks down **sugar** / **starch**.

Q2 The diagram below shows a starch and amylase mixture. You can use **iodine solution** to test if starch is present in the mixture. Once starch is no longer present, the reaction is complete.

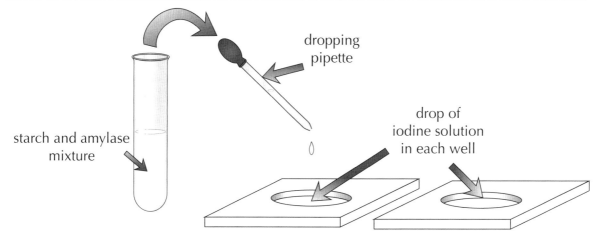

dropping pipette

drop of iodine solution in each well

starch and amylase mixture

Tick the correct box to show the colour of **iodine solution** when:

a) Starch is present.

brown-orange ☐
blue-black ☐
pink-purple ☐

b) Starch is no longer present.

brown-orange ☐
blue-black ☐
pink-purple ☐

Q3 To measure enzyme activity you choose which **variable** to change. Complete the table to give an example of how you could measure each variable. Temperature has been done for you.

Variable	How to measure it
Temperature	Put the test tubes into water baths at a range of temperatures.
pH	
Substrate concentration	

<u>*More on Enzyme Activity*</u>

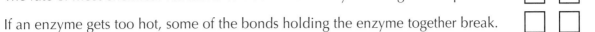

Q1 Tick the correct boxes to show whether the sentences are **true** or **false**.

                                                                    True False

a) The rate of most chemical reactions can be increased by lowering the temperature. ☐ ☐

b) If an enzyme gets too hot, some of the bonds holding the enzyme together break. ☐ ☐

c) Most enzymes in the human body work best at 37 °C. ☐ ☐

d) 'Denatured' means an enzyme is destroyed but it will go back to its normal shape. ☐ ☐

Q2 The graph below shows the results from an investigation into the effect of **temperature** on the rate of reaction.

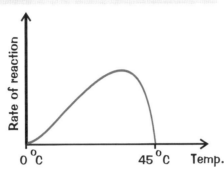

a) What is meant by an enzyme's **optimum** temperature?

....

....

b) Draw a cross on the graph to show the enzyme's optimum temperature.

Q3 The graph below shows how the **rate** of reaction is affected by **substrate concentration**.

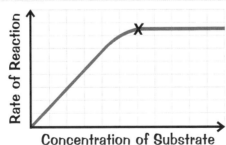

Complete the following sentences by circling the correct word from each pair.

a) The **higher** / **lower** the substrate concentration, the faster the reaction.

b) This is because there are **more** / **fewer** substrate molecules for the enzyme to react with.

c) After point X, the graph levels off because there are so many substrate molecules that all the active sites are **denatured** / **full**.

More on Enzyme Activity

Q4   Stuart has a sample of an enzyme and he is trying to find out what its **optimum pH** is.
Stuart tests the enzyme by **timing** how long it takes to break down a substance at
different pH levels. The results of Stuart's experiment are shown below.

pH	Time taken for reaction (seconds)
2	100
4	85
6	15
8	75
10	100
12	105

a)   Draw a line graph of the results on the grid below.

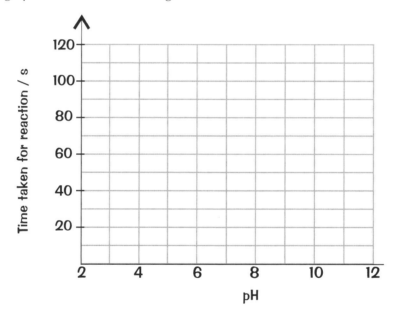

b)   Roughly what is the **optimum** pH for the enzyme?

....

c)   The stomach is very acidic. Would you expect to find this enzyme in the stomach?

....

d)   Describe two things that Stuart would need to do to make sure his experiment is a fair test.

1. ....

2. ....

Top Tips: Enzymes crop up a lot in Biology so it's worth spending plenty of time making sure
you know all the basics. Check that you know what 'active site', 'denatured' and 'optimum' mean.

Genetic Engineering

Q1 **Genetic engineering** uses enzymes to cut and paste genes.
The steps in this process are shown below. Put them in the correct
order by numbering the boxes. The first one has been done for you.

A useful gene is "cut" out from one organism's chromosome using enzymes. `1`

This produces a genetically modified (GM) organism. ☐

Enzymes are used to insert the useful gene from one organism's
chromosome into another organism's chromosome. ☐

Enzymes are used to cut another organism's chromosome. ☐

Q2 Tick the boxes to show whether the following statements are **true** or **false**.

		True	False
a)	Genetic engineering can be used to make human insulin.	☐	☐
b)	Viruses are genetically modified to make human insulin.	☐	☐
c)	All people think genetic engineering is totally safe.	☐	☐
d)	Human insulin can be made quickly and cheaply to treat diabetes.	☐	☐
e)	Genetic engineering can be used to decrease crop yield.	☐	☐
f)	Genetic engineering may create 'superweeds'.	☐	☐

Q3 The passage below is about **Golden Rice**.
Fill in the gaps in the passage using the words in the box.

> deficiency   organisms   GM   beta-carotene   fewer

Vitamin A .... means you don't get enough vitamin A. It can
make you go blind. .... is used by our bodies to make vitamin A.
Golden Rice is a type of .... rice. It contains genes from other
.... These genes allow Golden Rice to produce beta-carotene.
Growing Golden Rice could mean .... people will suffer from
vitamin A deficiency.

B2 Topic 1 — Genes and Enzymes

Genetic Engineering

Q4 A crop plant had been genetically modified to make it **resistant to herbicides**.

a) Explain how making a crop resistant to herbicides can help a farmer.

....

....

b) Some people were concerned that, as a result, wild grasses growing nearby might also become resistant to herbicides. Scientists decided to check whether this had happened.

The scientists sprayed herbicide onto 100 plants in an area next to the GM crop, and onto 100 plants from a second area far away from the GM crop.

Their results are shown in the table below.

Number of grass plants dying after spraying	
In area next to GM crop	In area far away from GM crop
83	85

i) Why did the scientists test a group of plants that had **not** been growing near the GM crop?

....

ii) How could the scientists have made the results of this experiment more reliable?

....

c) The scientists decided that there was no significant difference between the two groups of plants. Circle the statement below that you agree most with.

Their conclusion is incorrect. Only 83 plants died in the area next to the GM crop compared to 85.

Their conclusion is correct. A difference of 2 plants out of 100 could be due to chance.

d) If the scientists are right in their conclusion, does this prove that GM crops are totally safe?

....

e) Give a reason for your answer to part **d)**.

Remember, the scientists have only done one experiment.

....

....

Mitosis

Q1 Tick the boxes to show whether the following statements are **true** or **false**.

True False

a) Human body cells are diploid. ☐ ☐

b) Diploid means that there are three copies of each chromosome. ☐ ☐

c) There are 20 pairs of chromosomes in a human cell. ☐ ☐

d) One copy of each chromosome comes from the person's mother. ☐ ☐

e) Mitosis is where a cell divides to make two cells identical to the original cell. ☐ ☐

f) Organisms use mitosis in order to grow. ☐ ☐

g) Organisms do not use mitosis to replace damaged cells. ☐ ☐

Q2 a) The diagram on the right shows a cell which is about to divide by **mitosis**. In the space below, draw the cells that are produced when this cell divides.

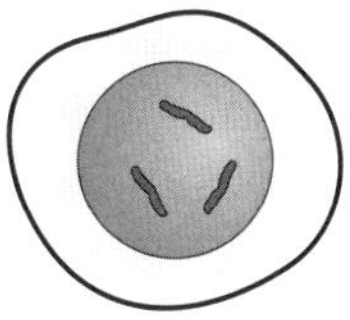

b) Complete the sentences below by circling the correct answers.

i) Mitosis produces **two / three / four** new cells.

ii) The new cells are **haploid / diploid**.

iii) The cells contain **exactly the same DNA / completely different DNA**.

Q3 Complete the following passage using the words below.

runners   strawberry   variation   asexual   reproduce   genes

Some organisms .... by mitosis. For example, ...
plants form .... using mitosis. These become new plants. This is an
example of .... reproduction. The offspring have exactly the same
.... as the parent. This means there's no genetic ....

Meiosis

Q1   Circle the correct word from each pair to complete the sentences below.

a)   Gametes are sex cells. They're called ova in **males** / **females** and sperm in **males** / **females**.

b)   During **asexual** / **sexual** reproduction, two gametes combine to form a new cell.

c)   Gametes are **diploid** / **haploid**. This means they have **one copy** / **two copies** of each chromosome.

d)   When two gametes combine, the resulting cell (called a zygote) has the right number
of chromosomes. Zygotes are **diploid** / **haploid**.

Q2   The diagram below shows two gametes combining at **fertilisation**. Use the words in the box
to label the diagram. The egg and its number of chromosomes has been labelled for you.

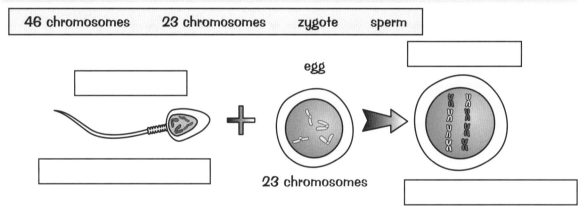

| 46 chromosomes | 23 chromosomes | zygote | sperm |

Q3   Tick the boxes to show whether the following statements are **true** or **false**.

                                                                                                              True False

a)   Meiosis halves the number of chromosomes. ☐ ☐

b)   Meiosis forms gametes that are genetically identical. ☐ ☐

c)   In humans, meiosis only happens in the reproductive organs. ☐ ☐

d)   Meiosis produces six haploid gametes. ☐ ☐

Q4   The stages of **meiosis** are listed below. Put them in the correct order
by numbering the boxes. The first one has been done for you.

☐   The cell divides. Some of the father's chromosomes and
some of the mother's chromosomes go into each new cell.

☐   You end up with four haploid gametes.

[1]   The DNA is copied to make X-shaped chromosomes.

☐   Each cell divides again. The X-shaped chromosomes are pulled apart.

Top Tips: It's easy to get confused between **mitosis** and **meiosis**. Mitosis produces cells for
growth and replaces damaged cells. Meiosis is for sexual reproduction and creates gametes.

Cloning Mammals

Q1 Complete each of the statements about **cloning** below by circling the correct words.

a) Cloning is a type of **asexual** / **sexual** reproduction.

b) Cloning produces cells that are genetically **different from** / **identical to** the original cell.

Q2 Cloning mammals has some **advantages**. Circle **three** reasons why humans might want to clone mammals.

Cloning animals is easy and fast.

Cloning increases the number of different alleles in the gene pool.

Studying animal clones could improve our understanding of things like ageing.

Cloning could be used to help preserve endangered species.

Cloning could help with the shortage of organs for transplants.

Clones are always born without any genetic defects.

Q3 Cloning mammals also has **disadvantages**.

a) Only **one** of the following statements is true. Tick the correct one.

Cloned animals are usually smaller than normal animals. ☐

There's a possibility that cloned animals might not live as long as normal animals. ☐

The cloning process never fails. ☐

b) Cloning mammals leads to a reduced gene pool, meaning there are fewer different alleles in a population.

i) What problem could this cause?

....

ii) Explain your answer to part **i)**.

....

....

c) Give **one** other problem associated with cloning animals.

....

....

Stem Cells

Q1 Tick the correct boxes to show whether the following statements are **true** or **false**.

		True	False
a)	To start with, the cells in an embryo are all the same. They are called embryonic stem cells.	☐	☐
b)	Blood cells are an example of a specialised cell.	☐	☐
c)	Adult stem cells are just as useful as embryonic stem cells.	☐	☐
d)	Adult humans don't have any stem cells in their bone marrow.	☐	☐
e)	Most animal cells lose the ability to differentiate at an early stage.	☐	☐
f)	Lots of plant cells lose the ability to differentiate at an early stage.	☐	☐
g)	The process of cells becoming specialised is called differentiation.	☐	☐

Q2 Scientists in the UK are carrying out research into the use of stem cells in **medicine**.

Complete the following passage using the words below.

damaged   adult   embryos   differentiate   replace

Doctors already use .... stem cells to cure some diseases. Scientists have

experimented with taking stem cells from very early human .... and

growing them. Under certain conditions these stem cells will .... into

specialised cells. It might be possible to create specialised cells to ....

those which have been .... by disease or injury.

Q3 People have **different opinions** when it comes to embryonic **stem cell research**.

a) Give one argument **in favour** of stem cell research.

....

....

b) Give one argument **against** stem cell research.

....

....

Top Tips: Stem cell research is a tricky one — any research that uses embryos is going to raise issues. It's a good idea to listen to all the arguments on both sides so you can work out what you think.

Mixed Questions — B2 Topic 1

Q1   Your **DNA** carries the **instructions** that tell your cells how to make **proteins**.

a)   The sequence of bases in part of one strand of a DNA molecule is as follows:

A–A–T–C–C–A–A–T–C

One of the boxes below shows the correct sequence of bases on the other strand of DNA.
Tick the correct box.

G–T–A–C–G–A–T–A–G   ☐   T–T–A–C–G–T–A–A–G   ☐   T–T–A–G–G–T–T–A–G   ☐

b)   Name the **two people** who built the first accurate model of the structure of DNA.

....

c)   Complete each of the following statements about DNA by circling the correct words.

   i)   A DNA molecule is made up of **two** / **three** strands of DNA coiled into a **double** / **triple** helix.

   ii) The strands are held together by **covalent bonds** / **hydrogen bonds** between pairs of bases.

   iii) Adenine always pairs with **thymine** / **cytosine** and guanine always pairs with **thymine** / **cytosine**.

Q2   **Stem cells** may be able to cure many diseases.

a)   What unique characteristic do **stem cells** have which ordinary body cells don't have?
Circle the correct answer.

      Stem cells never mutate.   Stem cells can only ever become one type of cell.   Stem cells can differentiate into specialised cells.

b)   Scientists have experimented with growing stem cells in different conditions.

   i)   What is the name of the process by which stem cells **divide** for growth?

   ....

   ii) Complete this sentence about the process you named in part **i)** by circling the correct word.

   This process makes two cells that are genetically **identical** / **different** to the original cell.

B2 Topic 1 — Genes and Enzymes

Mixed Questions — B2 Topic 1

Q3 Tick the correct boxes to show whether the following statements are **true** or **false**.

		True	False
a)	Bacterial cells have a nucleus.	☐	☐
b)	Animal cells have a large vacuole.	☐	☐
c)	Plasmids are small loops of extra DNA.	☐	☐
d)	Franklin and Wilkins worked out that DNA had a helical structure.	☐	☐
e)	Enzymes are all proteins.	☐	☐
f)	The lock and key mechanism is to do with mitosis.	☐	☐
g)	Amylase is an enzyme that breaks down starch.	☐	☐

Q4 a) A scientist is studying the different types of **cell division**.
Tick the box to show whether the statement relates to **mitosis** or **meiosis**.

		Mitosis	Meiosis
i)	Is used for growth and repair.	☐	☐
ii)	Produces four gametes.	☐	☐
iii)	Produces gametes with only one copy of each chromosome in it.	☐	☐
iv)	Only happens in the reproductive organs.	☐	☐
v)	Produces genetically different cells.	☐	☐
vi)	Produces diploid cells.	☐	☐
vii)	Produces haploid cells.	☐	☐

b) The scientist views a dividing cell under a light microscope.
The actual cell is **0.001 cm** wide.
The image of the cell is **0.8 cm** wide.
Calculate the magnification of the image.

$$\text{magnification} = \frac{\text{length of image}}{\text{length of specimen}}$$

....

....

magnification = × ....

c) If the scientist wants to see the cell in **more detail**, what type of microscope should he use?

....

Respiration

Q1 Part of the **word equation** for one type of **respiration** is shown below.

a) Complete the equation for respiration.

.... + oxygen → carbon dioxide + ... (+ energy)

b) What type of respiration is this? Circle the correct answer.

Aerobic respiration   **Anaerobic respiration**

c) Which of these statements is **not** true of respiration? Underline the correct answer.

It is used by all living organisms.   It releases energy from food.

It is another word for breathing.   It can be aerobic or anaerobic.

Q2 Draw lines to match the **body part** or **process** to the correct description.

capillaries

circulatory system

diffusion

digestive system

Breaks down the food source needed for respiration.

The movement of particles from an area of higher concentration to an area of lower concentration.

Really tiny blood vessels.

The system that carries glucose, oxygen and carbon dioxide around your body in the blood.

Q3 The diagram shows **blood** passing through **muscle tissue**.

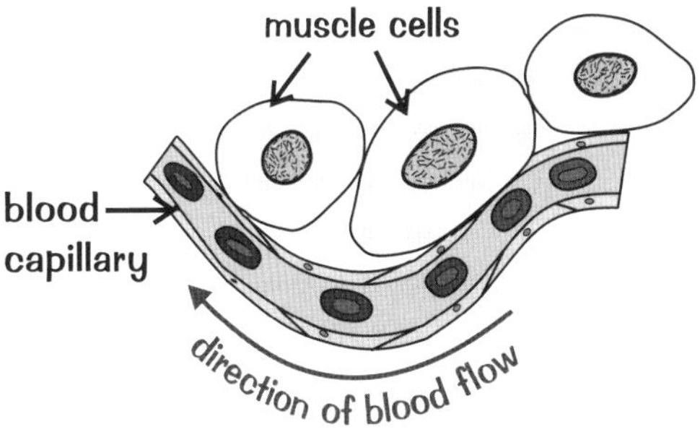

Complete the following passage about substances moving into and out of the blood using the words below.

muscle cells

blood capillary

direction of blood flow

cells   respire   blood   diffuse
blood   higher   cells

When cells ...., they use up oxygen and glucose. There's a higher

concentration of oxygen and glucose in the .... than in the

.... So oxygen and glucose .... from the blood into

the cells. When cells respire they produce lots of carbon dioxide. There's a

.... concentration of carbon dioxide in the cells than in the blood.

So carbon dioxide diffuses from the .... into the ....

Respiration and Exercise

Q1 Humans can respire **aerobically** — if there isn't enough oxygen available we can also respire **anaerobically**.

Tick the boxes to show whether the following statements are **true** or **false**.

		True	False
a)	Anaerobic respiration releases more energy than aerobic respiration.	☐	☐
b)	Aerobic respiration produces a build-up of lactic acid in the muscles.	☐	☐
c)	We use anaerobic respiration when we are walking slowly.	☐	☐

Q2 a) In what circumstances would a human start respiring **anaerobically**? Circle the correct answer.

when asleep   when there's not enough oxygen available   when jogging gently

b) Complete the **word equation** for anaerobic respiration in humans.

glucose → .... (+ energy)

Q3 Joe investigated how **exercise** affects his **heart rate**. He took his **pulse** after **sitting still** for five minutes, after **walking** for five minutes and after **running** for five minutes. Joe's results are shown on the graph on the right.

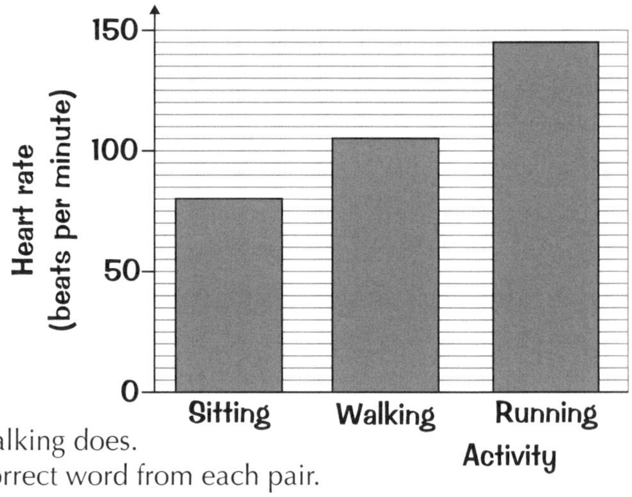

a) What is Joe's heart rate when sitting still?

.... beats per minute

b) Running increases Joe's heart rate more than walking does. Complete the sentence below by circling the correct word from each pair.

When Joe exercises, his body needs to get more **oxygen** / **carbon dioxide** to the muscles

and take more **oxygen** / **carbon dioxide** away from the muscles.

c) Joe has a **stroke volume** of 65 cm³. Use your answer to part **a)** to calculate Joe's **cardiac output** when he is **sitting still**.

cardiac output = heart rate × stroke volume

....

....

.... cm³ per minute

Respiration and Exercise

Q4 Jim is a keen runner. He takes part in a 400 metre race. The **graph** below shows Jim's **breathing rate** before, during and after the race.

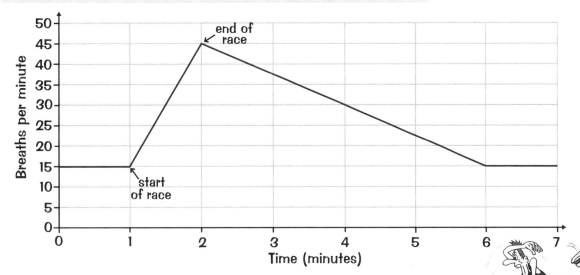

a) By how much has Jim's breathing rate gone up by the end of the race?

.... breaths per minute

b) How long does it take Jim to recover (for his breathing rate to return to normal) after the race?

.... minutes

c) The passage below describes how Jim's body responds to the race.
Complete the sentences using the words below.

quickly	anaerobically	muscles	cramp	EPOC
oxygen	lactic acid	'repay'	hurt	energy

i) During the run, Jim's breathing rate increases. This is so he can get more

.... into his blood. When Jim exercises, his ....

contract, so he needs more ....

ii) As he gets to the end of the race, Jim's muscles start to .... This is

because his body can't supply oxygen to his muscles .... enough,

so they start respiring .... This type of respiration produces a

build-up of .... in the muscles. This gets painful and can give you

....

iii) After the race, it takes a while for Jim's breathing rate to return to normal. This is

because he has to .... the oxygen which he didn't manage to get to

his muscles in time. The amount of oxygen needed is called the excess post-exercise

oxygen consumption (..................................).

Photosynthesis

Q1 Circle the correct word(s) in each pair to complete the passage below.

> Leaves are full of little holes called stomata. They open and close
>
> to let **carbon dioxide** / **oxygen** in and **carbon dioxide** / **oxygen** out.
>
> They also allow water vapour to **enter** / **escape**.

Q2 **Photosynthesis** is the process that produces 'food' in plants. Use the words from the box below to complete the equation for photosynthesis. One has been done for you.

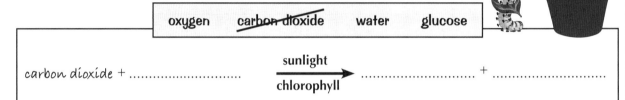

| oxygen | carbon dioxide | water | glucose |

carbon dioxide + ... $\xrightarrow[\text{chlorophyll}]{\text{sunlight}}$ .... + ...

Q3 Tick the boxes to show whether the following statements are **true** or **false**.

True False

a) Photosynthesis happens inside the chloroplasts. ☐ ☐

b) Photosynthesis happens in all plant cells. ☐ ☐

c) Plants absorb carbon dioxide from the air. ☐ ☐

d) Mitochondria contain chlorophyll. ☐ ☐

e) Sunlight provides the energy for photosynthesis. ☐ ☐

Q4 The diagram below shows one way of measuring the rate of photosynthesis. Circle the most appropriate word(s) from each pair to complete the following statements.

a) When photosynthesis is taking place **quickly** / **slowly**, more bubbles of gas are produced.

b) You can measure the rate of photosynthesis by counting the bubbles of **oxygen** / **carbon dioxide** produced by some pondweed in a given time.

bubbles of gas
pondweed

Top Tips: If green plants couldn't trap the Sun's energy, that would pretty much be the end of life on Earth — and certainly of us. So why not go and hug a tree now to say thanks...

B2 Topic 2 — Life Processes

Photosynthesis

Q5 A diagram of a leaf in cross-section is shown below.

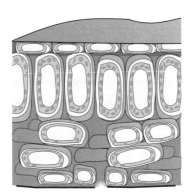

Circle the correct option to show how the following features of the leaf are important.

a) The leaf has a **broad surface**.

This means that there's a large surface area for insects to land on.

This means that there's a large surface area for light to fall on.

b) The leaf contains lots of **chloroplasts**.

This means that the leaf can absorb lots of light for photosynthesis.

This means that the leaf can absorb lots of oxygen for respiration.

Q6 Below are some more questions about **photosynthesis**. Hooray.

a) Certain factors stop photosynthesis from going any faster. What is the name given to these factors? Tick the correct box.

☐ Limiting factors   ☐ Speed factors   ☐ Reducing factors

b) Circle **three** things that can stop photosynthesis from going any faster.

temperature   light intensity   nitrogen concentration

wind speed   carbon dioxide concentration   oxygen concentration

c) The rate of photosynthesis at a particular time depends on the environmental conditions, e.g. season (such as winter). Name **two** other environmental conditions that may affect the rate of photosynthesis.

1. ....

2. ....

The Rate of Photosynthesis

Q1 Lucy investigated the **volume of oxygen** produced by pondweed at **different intensities of light**. Her results are shown in the table below.

Relative light intensity	1	2	3	4	5
Vol. of O_2 produced in 10 mins (ml)	12	25	13	48	61

bubbles of oxygen
pondweed

a) Plot a graph of her results. One point has been plotted for you.

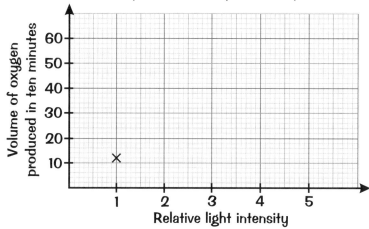

b) One of Lucy's results is probably wrong. Circle this point on the graph.

c) Circle the statement below that describes the relationship shown on the graph.

> The rate of photosynthesis decreased as light intensity increased.

> The rate of photosynthesis increased as light intensity increased.

Q2 Seth investigated the effect of different levels of **carbon dioxide** on the rate of photosynthesis of his Swiss cheese plant. The results are shown on the graph.

Complete the passage using the words in the box below to explain the relationship between the level of carbon dioxide and the rate of photosynthesis.

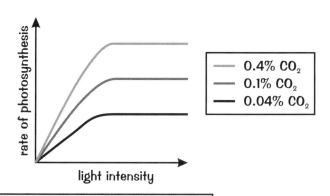

temperature	point	limiting	light	increases

Increasing the level of carbon dioxide .... the rate of photosynthesis, but

only up to a .... After this the graph flattens out. This shows that carbon

dioxide is no longer the .... factor. As long as there's enough carbon

dioxide and .... then the limiting factor must be ....

The Rate of Photosynthesis

Q3 Average **daytime summer temperatures** in different habitats around the world are shown in the table below.

Habitat	Temperature (°C)
Forest	19
Arctic	0
Desert	32
Grassland	22
Rainforest	27

a) Plot a **bar chart** of these results on the grid below.

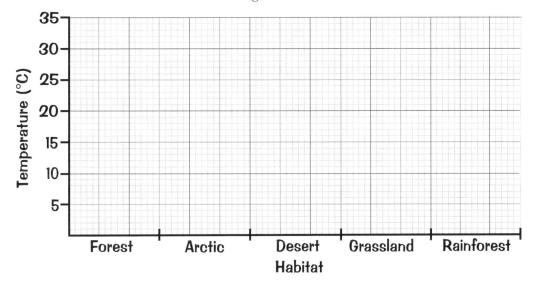

b) From the values for temperature, in which area would you expect **fewest** plants to grow?

....

c) Suggest a reason for your answer to part **b)**.

....

....

Use the words <u>enzymes</u> and <u>photosynthesis</u> in your answer.

....

....

d) Many plant species grow in the rainforest. Very few plants grow in the desert, even though it has a much higher average temperature than the rainforest. Suggest a reason for this.

....

Top Tips: You might get asked to draw a graph in your exam, or join some points on a graph. If so, make sure you always use a <u>sharp pencil</u> to draw a clear, crisp line. No **thick lines** allowed.

Osmosis

Q1 Use the words from the box below to complete the definition for osmosis.

> low   high   water molecules

Osmosis is the movement of .... across a partially

permeable membrane from a region of .... water

concentration to a region of .... water concentration.

Q2 This diagram shows a tank separated into two by a partially permeable membrane.

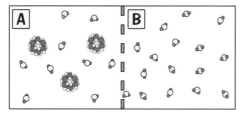

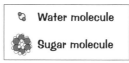

a) On which side of the membrane is there the higher concentration of water molecules?

....

b) In which direction would you expect **more** water molecules to travel — from A to B or from B to A?

....

Q3 Some **potato cylinders** were placed in solutions of different **salt concentrations**. At the start of the experiment each cylinder was 50 mm long. Their final lengths are recorded in the table below.

Concentration of salt (molar)	Final length of cylinder (mm)	Change in length of cylinder (mm)
0	60	+10
0.25	58	
0.5	56	
0.75	54	
1	50	

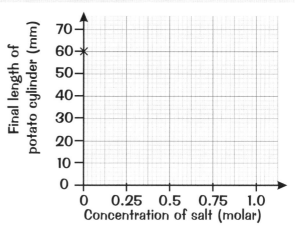

a) Plot the points for concentration of salt solution vs final length of potato cylinders on the grid. The first one has been done for you.

b) Work out the change in length of each of the cylinders and complete the table above. The first one has been done for you.

c) Look at the pattern of results. What do they show?

....

....

Water Uptake and Loss in Plants

Q1   Flowering plants have **tube networks** for moving substances around.

a) Name the vessels that carry **sugars** around the plant. ....

b) Circle the correct word from each pair to complete the following sentence.

> Sugars are transported from the **roots** / **leaves** (where they are made) to parts of the
> plant that are **growing** / **dying** and to the plant's **storage** / **protective** tissues.

Q2   The diagram below is of the **transpiration stream**.
Complete the passage using the words in the box.

stream	evaporates	roots	shortage	xylem

a) Water .... from the leaves.

b) This creates a slight .... of water in the leaf. More water is drawn up from the rest of the plant through the .... vessels to replace it.

c) This in turn means more water is drawn up from the ....

d) This means there's a constant .... of water through the plant.

Q3   A diagram of a **cell** found in the **root** of a **plant** is shown on the right.

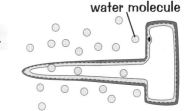
water molecule

a) Name the type of cell shown. ....

b) Why does this type of cell have the particular shape shown?

....

c) On the diagram, draw an arrow to show the **net movement** of water molecules.

d) Roots also absorb minerals from the soil. The concentration of minerals in the soil is usually low.

    i) Name the process by which roots absorb minerals. ....

    ii) Why does this process require energy?

....

Distribution — Pooters and Pitfall Traps

Q1 Tick the boxes to show whether the following statements are **true** or **false**.

True False

a) A habitat is the place where an organism lives. ☐ ☐

b) The distribution of an organism is how an organism interacts with its habitat. ☐ ☐

c) To study the distribution of an organism you can measure how common
it is in two sample areas and compare them. ☐ ☐

Q2 Circle the correct word(s) from each pair to complete the following statements.

a) You would use a pitfall trap to investigate the distribution
of **ground insects** / **pond animals**.

b) The top of a pitfall trap is **completely covered** / **partly open**.

c) The sides of a pitfall trap are **steep** / **shallow** so that insects that fall
into it **can** / **can't** get out again.

Q3 Mark wants to compare the distribution of beetles in two different areas.
He decides to collect the beetles using a **pooter**.

a) Complete the passage to explain how to use a pooter to compare
the distribution of beetles. Use the words in the box below.

| count | sucked | shorter | compare | crawl |

Suck on the .... tube of the pooter. Put the longer end over

a beetle and it'll be .... into a jar. In your first sample area,

.... around for a few minutes sucking up as many beetles as

you can. Then .... the number of beetles you've collected.

Do this in your second sample area and .... what you find.

b) Name **two** things Mark needs to keep the same both times to make sure his test is fair.

1. ....

2. ....

Top Tips: Exam questions on distribution are pretty common. In fact I'd say there's about the
same chance of them coming up as there is of finding some insects in your garden (pretty high)...

Distribution — Nets and Quadrats

Q1 Sweep nets are used to collect insects. Underline **three** statements about sweep nets that are **true**.

A sweep net is a net lined with strong cloth.

It is used for collecting insects from long grass.

It is used for collecting insects from underground.

You must stand still when using a sweep net.

A sweep net is a brush with a sticky net on it.

You must run around as fast as you can when using a sweep net.

Q2 Sally sampled the population of **water snails** in two ponds.

a) Name a piece of equipment that Sally might have used to collect the snails.

....

b) Sally sampled each pond **three** times.
The table below shows her results. Complete the table by filling in the mean numbers of snails.

$$\text{Mean} = \frac{\text{total number of snails}}{\text{number of samples}}$$

	Sample 1	Sample 2	Sample 3	Mean number of snails
Pond 1	2 snails	6 snails	7 snails	
Pond 2	10 snails	9 snails	14 snails	

Q3 Alex is comparing how many daisies are in two different sample areas.

She uses a random number generator to pick coordinates to place her quadrat. Alex's friend Richard completes the same experiment but he puts his quadrat wherever he sees the most daisies.

a) Whose results are more reliable, **Alex's** or **Richard's**?

....

b) Explain your answer to part **a)**.

....

....

c) If Alex was to repeat her experiment again, how could she make her results more reliable?

....

More on Distribution

Q1   **Environmental factors** can affect how organisms are **distributed**.
Draw lines to match the **environmental factor** to how you could measure it.

| light intensity | | an electronic pH monitor |

temperature   an electronic device called a light sensor

soil pH   a thermometer

Q2   Some students wanted to estimate the size of the population of **clover plants** around their school.

a) The school field is 250 m long by 180 m wide.

   i) What is the area of the school field?

.... m²

   ii) Hannah counted 11 clover plants in a 1 m² area of the field.
Approximately how many clover plants are there likely to be on the whole field?

....

....

....

population size = total area × mean number of plants

b) Lisa decided to collect data from five different 1 m² areas of the school field and work out the mean. Her results are shown in the table below.

	Area 1	Area 2	Area 3	Area 4	Area 5	Mean
No. of plants	11	9	8	9	7	8.8

Use Lisa's data and your answer to **a) i)** to estimate the population size of clover plants on the field.

....

....

c) Whose estimation of population size is likely to be more accurate? Explain your answer.

....

....

Top Tips: Some questions may feel like you're doing maths rather than biology... but you can't get away from things like means — you do need to know how to work them out for the exam. Booo.

Mixed Questions — B2 Topic 2

Q1   Humans can respire **aerobically** and **anaerobically**.

a)   Complete the definition of respiration using the words in the box.

| energy | cell | glucose |

Respiration is the process of breaking down .... to

release ...., which goes on in every living ....

b)   Circle the correct word(s) from each pair to complete the following sentences.

Anaerobic respiration happens when there's not enough **oxygen** / **carbon dioxide** available.

It produces a build up of **lactic acid** / **glucose** in the muscles.

More / **Less** energy is released during anaerobic respiration than during aerobic respiration.

c)   Anaerobic respiration is not as efficient as aerobic respiration. Why is it still useful to us?
Tick the correct box.

☐   It doesn't produce an oxygen debt.

☐   It allows the body to keep going longer in emergencies.

Q2   The diagram shows a **plant**, A, growing in a **tropical rainforest**.

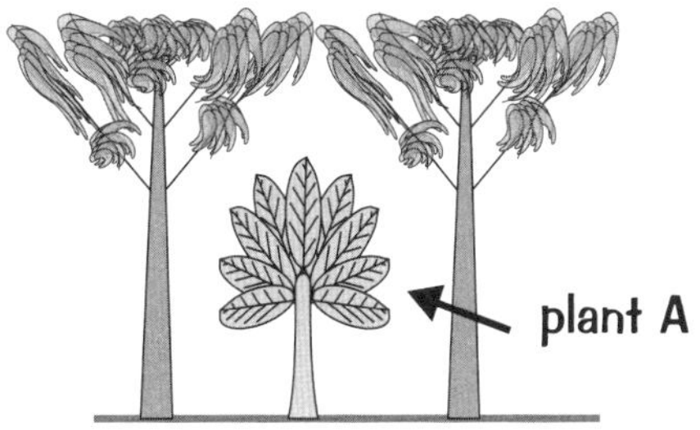

plant A

a)   Which factor is most likely to limit the rate of photosynthesis in plant A? Circle the right answer.

the amount of carbon dioxide   the amount of light   the temperature

b)   Explain your answer to part **a)**.

....

c)   Plant A needs to take in water to keep photosynthesising.
Tick the name of the vessel that carries water from the plant's roots to its leaves.

☐ phloem   ☐ xylem

Mixed Questions — B2 Topic 2

Q3 A student was given **three solutions** labelled X, Y and Z. He set up the experiment shown on the right and left it for a day. At the end of the experiment, the water outside the membrane contained particles **X** and **Y**, but **not Z**.

solutions X, Y and Z

water

a) By which process have particles X and Y moved through the membrane? Circle the correct answer.

active transport   osmosis   diffusion

b) Which particles do you think are the **largest**, X, Y or Z? ☐

c) Give a reason for your answer to part **b**).

....

....

d) During the experiment, some **water** particles moved from the beaker into the membrane. Name the process the water particles moved by. ....

Q4 Eve and Bill work together to study the **distribution** of **harebells** in a meadow. They each pick a **sample area** and use a **quadrat** to estimate the population size.

Harebells are pretty little blue flowers.

a) The results of Bill and Eve's investigation are shown in the table on the right.

Fill in the two means in the results table.

	Number of harebells				
	Quadrat 1	Quadrat 2	Quadrat 3	Quadrat 4	Mean
Bill's area	5	7	2	4	
Eve's Area	8	11	9	12	

b) Eve has read that harebells grow best in **acidic soil**. She wonders if that's why there are more harebells in her area.

i) Suggest a piece of equipment that Eve could use to test the acidity of the soil.

....

ii) If the pH of the soil is low, does this support her hypothesis?

....

c) Eve wants to know how the distribution of harebells changes across the meadow. She marks out a line across the meadow and takes samples by moving the quadrat along the line. What is this method called?

....

d) Bill's friend Ben is studying the number of **spiders** in the meadow. The meadow is covered in **long grass**. Name a piece of equipment that Ben could use to collect spiders in the meadow.

....

Evidence for Evolution

Q1 Fossils were found in this sample of **rock**.

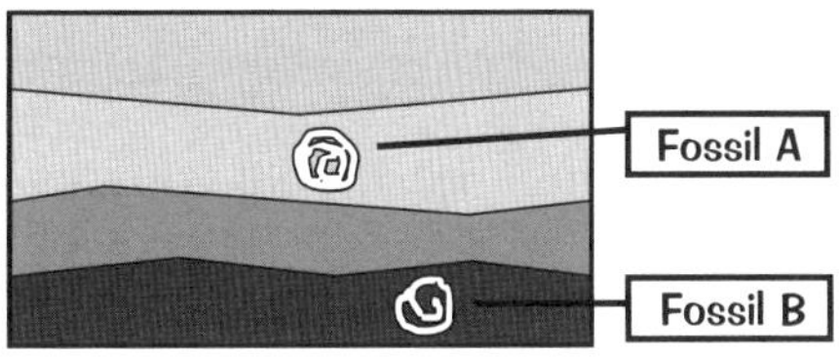

Fossil A
Fossil B

a) What is a fossil?
Tick the correct box.

☐ A rock from long ago.

☐ Any trace of an animal or plant that lived long ago.

☐ Any object dug out of the ground.

b) Circle **three** things that a fossil can tell us about organisms that lived long ago.

What they looked like.　　　What organism ate them.

How long ago they existed.　　What they did for fun.　　How they've evolved.

c) In the picture above, which is the oldest fossil? Tick the correct answer.

☐ Fossil A　　　　　　　☐ Fossil B

Q2 Circle the most appropriate word(s) from each pair to complete the following statements.

Fossils can be formed in three ways:

a) From **compressions** / **impressions** that have been left in
soft materials like **sand** / **clay**. E.g. footprints.

b) From the **hard** / **soft** bits of animals that don't easily **decay** / **get washed away**.
E.g. teeth, bones and shells.

c) From parts of organisms that **grow** / **don't decay** because the conditions aren't right
for **microbes** / **viruses** to work. E.g. in amber (where there's no oxygen or moisture).

Q3 The fossil record is **incomplete** — there are gaps in it.
Give **three reasons** why we do not have fossils of some organisms.

1. ....

2. ....

3. ....

Growth and Development

Q1 If an organism increases in size or mass, it is **growing**.

What is being measured if you measure:

a) An organism's mass including all the water in its body?

....

b) An organism's mass when it is dead and has been dried out?

....

Q2 Animals and plants **grow** in different ways.

a) Draw lines to match each of the **growth processes** below to its correct definition.

CELL ELONGATION   When one cell splits into two by mitosis.

CELL DIFFERENTIATION   Where a cell expands, making the cell bigger.

CELL DIVISION   The process where a cell changes to become specialised for its job.

b) Tick the boxes to show whether the following statements are about **plants** or **animals**.

                                                   Plants Animals

   i) Growth happens all the time. ☐ ☐

   ii) When full growth is reached, growth stops. ☐ ☐

   iii) Cell differentiation is lost an early stage. ☐ ☐

   iv) Growth in height is mainly due to cell elongation. ☐ ☐

Q3 A baby's growth was recorded. The results are shown on the **growth chart** on the right.

a) What was the baby's mass at 1 year? .... kg

b) The baby's growth was above the 25th percentile at 6 months. Explain what the 25th percentile shows.

....

....

Cell Organisation and the Circulatory System

Q1 Specialised cells form tissues, which form organs, which form organ systems. Draw lines to match the following words to their descriptions.

TISSUE

ORGAN

ORGAN SYSTEM

A group of different tissues that work together to perform a particular function.

A group of organs that work together to perform a function.

A group of similar cells that work together to carry out a particular function.

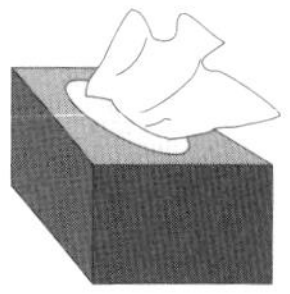

Q2 The diagram below shows the human **heart**, as seen from the front. Some parts have been labelled for you. Complete the remaining labels **a)** to **f)** using the words in the box.

aorta   vena cava   left ventricle   right atrium   valves   pulmonary vein

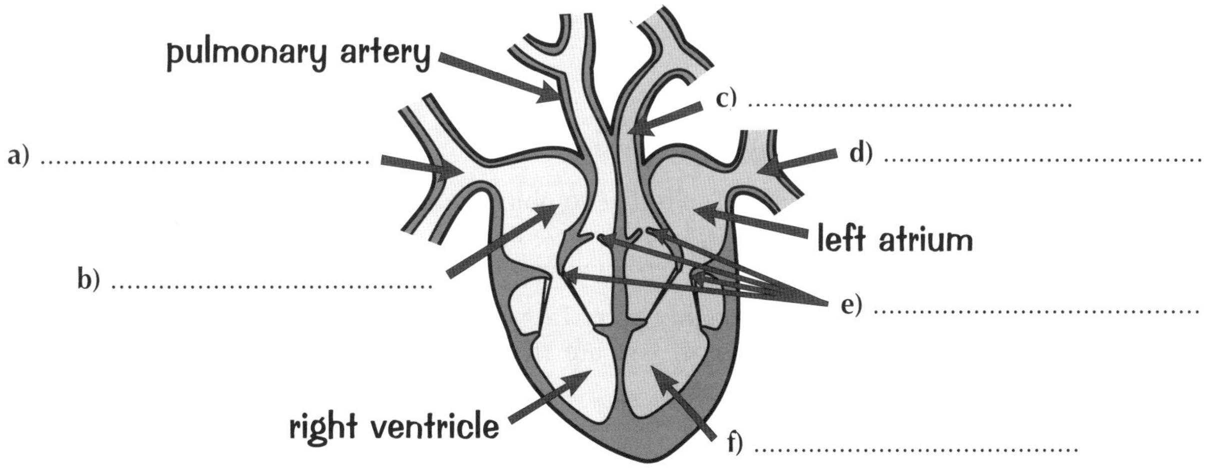

pulmonary artery

c) ....

a) ....

d) ....

left atrium

b) ....

e) ....

right ventricle

f) ....

Q3 Tick the boxes to say whether each statement below is **true** or **false**.

	True	False
a) The pulmonary vein pumps blood to the lungs.	☐	☐
b) The atria of the heart have thicker walls than the ventricles.	☐	☐
c) The right side of the heart pumps deoxygenated blood.	☐	☐
d) Valves prevent the backflow of blood.	☐	☐

The Circulatory System — The Blood

Q1 Which of these statements are **true** and which are **false**? Tick the correct boxes.

	True	False
a) The main job of red blood cells is to fight germs.	☐	☐
b) Glucose can be found in the blood.	☐	☐
c) The liquid part of blood is called urea.	☐	☐
d) Platelets help blood to clot at a wound.	☐	☐
e) Red blood cells don't have a nucleus.	☐	☐

Q2 Use the words below to complete the passage about white blood cells.

antitoxins	antibodies	shape	disease

White blood cells defend the body against ....

White blood cells can change .... to gobble up microorganisms.

They produce .... to fight microorganisms. They also produce

.... to get rid of any toxins produced by the microorganisms.

Q3 **Red blood cells** carry **oxygen** in the blood.

a) i) Name the substance in these cells that combines with oxygen. ....

ii) What shape are red blood cells? ....

b) Red blood cells are replaced roughly every 120 days. Approximately how many times per year are all the red blood cells in the body replaced?

Work out how many times 120 days goes into one year (365 days).

....

Q4 Plasma is the substance that carries everything in the blood. List four substances that are carried by plasma.

1. ....

2. ....

3. ....

4. ....

The Circulatory System — Blood Vessels

Q1 Draw lines to match each of the words below with its correct description.

artery   vessel that carries the blood away from the heart

capillary   vessel that carries the blood towards the heart

vein   vessel involved in the exchange of materials with tissues

Q2 Circle the correct word in each of the sentences below.

a) **Arteries / Veins** contain valves to keep the blood flowing in the right direction.

b) **Capillaries / Veins** have walls that are permeable.

c) **Arteries / Capillaries** have thick layers of muscle in their walls.

d) The blood pressure in the **arteries / veins** is higher than in the **arteries / veins**.

Q3 Gareth did an experiment to compare the elasticity of **arteries** and **veins**. He took out an artery and a vein from a piece of fresh meat. He then took a 5 cm length of each vessel, hung different masses on it, and measured how much it stretched. His results are shown in the table.

a) Suggest **one** way that Gareth could tell which was the artery and which was the vein when he was dissecting the meat.

....

....

b) Which vessel stretched more easily?

....

c) Why did he take both vessels from the same piece of meat?

....

....

mass added (g)	length of blood vessel (mm)	
	artery	vein
0	50	50
5	51	53
10	53	56
15	55	59
20	56	-

Top Tips: It's really important to remember the differences between arteries, veins and capillaries — don't get them mixed up. It's the kind of thing that crops up on exams all the time...

Peristalsis and Digestive Enzymes

Q1   During digestion, **enzymes** break **large molecules** down
into **smaller molecules** that can be absorbed by the body.

a)   Look at the list below. **Underline** all the large molecules. **Circle** all the small molecules.

amino acids   sugars   proteins   fatty acids

fats   glycerol   starch

b)   Name one example of a **carbohydrase** enzyme. ....

c)   What type of enzyme is **pepsin**? ....

Q2   Fill in the boxes using the words on the plate to show how the
three main food groups are **broken down** during digestion.

a)

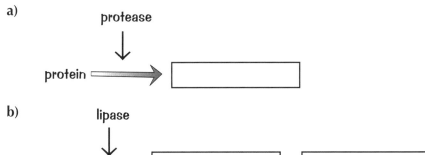

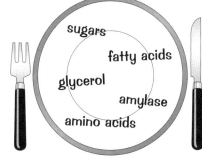

b)

c)

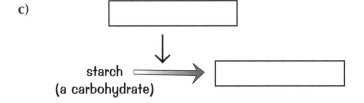

Q3   **Peristalsis** helps the food that we eat get to the stomach from the mouth.

The diagram below shows peristalsis happening in the gut. The longitudinal muscles are labelled.

a)   Label the **circular** muscles.

b)   Add an arrow to the diagram to show which way the food is travelling.

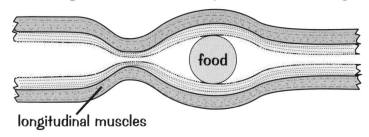

longitudinal muscles

The Digestive System

Q1   Complete this diagram of the human **digestive system** using the words in the box.

small intestine   oesophagus   pancreas
large intestine   mouth   liver   stomach

Q2   Number the boxes 1 to 4 to show the **order** that food passes through these parts of the **digestive system**.

☐ stomach   ☐ mouth

☐ large intestine   ☐ small intestine

Q3   Describe the **role** of each of the following in digestion:

a)   Oesophagus ....

....

b)   Pancreas ....

....

c)   Large intestine...

....

Investigating Digestive Enzymes

Q1 Jenny investigated how the concentration of an enzyme affects
the rate of digestion. She filled three pieces of visking tubing with
starch solution and different concentrations of the enzyme **amylase**.

a) Which of these statements are **true** and which are **false**? Tick the correct boxes. **True False**

   i) Visking tubing is a good model for the gut. ☐ ☐

   ii) Visking tubing lets big molecules through but not small ones. ☐ ☐

   iii) Visking tubing has the exact same length and surface area as your gut. ☐ ☐

   iv) Using visking tubing is cheaper and easier than using an animal's gut. ☐ ☐

b) Jenny put the pieces of visking tubing into three test tubes filled with distilled water, like this:

A   B   C

Visking tubing filled with starch and amylase

test tube filled with water

After four hours she tested the water outside each piece of tubing with Benedict's reagent.
Her results are shown in the table below.

Tube	Amylase concentration	Colour of Benedict's reagent
A	5 mol/dm^3	brick-red
B	0.5 mol/dm^3	yellow
C	2 mol/dm^3	orange

   i) Name the substance that Benedict's reagent is used as a test for. ....

   ii) State the colour of Benedict's reagent when none of this substance is present. ....

c) The passage below explains how enzyme concentration affects the rate of a reaction.
   Use the words in the box to fill in the gaps.

   colour   sugar   faster   amylase   starch

   The higher the concentration of ...., the more the Benedict's reagent

   has changed .... This means that more ....

   has been broken down to .... So the higher the concentration

   of an enzyme, the .... the rate of reaction.

Functional Foods

Q1 What is a 'functional food'? Tick the correct answer.

☐ A food that has some kind of health benefit beyond basic nutrition.

☐ A food that makes you more alert because it contains high levels of sugar and caffeine.

☐ A food that has extra vitamins and minerals added to it.

Q2 **Probiotics** are added to some foods.

a) Complete the passage about **probiotics** using the words in the box.

digestive	gut	bacteria	healthy

Probiotics are 'good' ...., which are similar to those found

naturally in your .... It is thought that they help to keep

your .... and immune system ....

b) Circle **one** example of a common probiotic food from the list below.

pasta   yogurts   ham

vegetables

c) Circle **two** examples of bacteria that are used in probiotic foods.

MRSA   Escherichia Coli

Lactobacillus

Streptococcus   Bifidobacteria
pyogenes

Q3 Some people take **prebiotic** supplements.

a) Which of these statements are **true** and which are **false**? Tick the correct boxes.

	True	False
i) Prebiotics are proteins we can't digest.	☐	☐
ii) It's thought that prebiotics can improve your digestive and immune systems.	☐	☐
iii) Prebiotics are a food supply for the 'good' bacteria found in your gut.	☐	☐

b) Name **one** food in which prebiotics are naturally found.

....

Top Tips: Some bacteria are 'bad' and can cause disease but there are also 'good' bacteria. Everyone has 'good' bacteria in their guts — they're really important for digestion. Some functional foods are designed to try to help the 'good' bacteria to grow and thrive. How very kind of them...

Functional Foods

Q4 Two reports were published about eating **probiotic yogurts**.

Report A was a magazine article published by the makers
of 'Well-U' probiotic yogurt. It was about two ordinary
women who ate two 'Well-U' yogurts every day for a week.

Report B appeared in a well-known science journal. It was a study in
which a trial group of 500 hospital patients were given a probiotic yogurt
for breakfast every day. A control group were given normal yogurt.

a) Which of these reports has used a more **reliable method** for investigating yogurts?
Tick the correct box.

□ Report A   □ Report B

b) Circle **three** reasons that support your answer to part **a)**.

It wasn't connected to the person selling the yogurt.

It was published in a magazine.

The study focused on two women who ate the yogurts.

It was published in a well-known science journal.

The study had a large sample size and used a control group.

It was connected to the person selling the yogurt.

Q5 Scientists did an experiment into the effectiveness of **stanol esters** in lowering people's **blood cholesterol**. They asked two groups of 100 people each to use a special spread instead of butter. Group A's spread was based on vegetable oil. Group B's spread was exactly the same, except that it contained large amounts of stanol esters. The cholesterol levels of each group were measured before the start of the experiment, and again after six months. The results are shown in the table.

	Group A / units	Group B / units
Mean blood cholesterol at start	6.3	6.4
Mean blood cholesterol after 6 mths	6.1	5.5

a) Which group was the **control** group in this experiment, **A** or **B**? ....

b) The scientists wanted the two groups of people to be as similar as possible.
For example, they chose people who were all a similar age.
Give **one** other example of something that should be similar in both groups.

....

c) Why was blood cholesterol measured before the experiment as well as at the end?

....

Mixed Questions — B2 Topic 3

Q1 **Growth** can involve cells **dividing**, **elongating** or **differentiating**.

a) **Plant growth** differs from **animal growth**. Complete the passage below using the words in the box.

| elongation | division | young | roots | differentiate | repair | lost |

i) Growth in animals happens by cell .... Animals tend to grow

while they're .... then reach full growth and stop growing.

Most cell division in adult males is for ....

Cell differentiation is .... at an early stage.

ii) Growth in plants happens all the time. Plants .... to develop

new parts. Growth in height is mainly due to cell ....

Cell division usually just happens in the tips of the .... and shoots.

b) Cells differentiate to become specialised cells, which form **tissues**. Describe what a **tissue** is.

....

c) A group of different tissues work together to perform a particular function.

What is this group of tissues called? ....

Q2 Enzymes are really important in the **digestive process**.

a) Which enzyme is responsible for the digestion of fats?

☐ Carbohydrase ☐ Amylase ☐ Lipase

b) Draw lines to match the area of the digestive system to what happens there.

MOUTH

STOMACH

SMALL INTESTINE

Food is pummelled by muscular walls.

Enzymes are added and food is absorbed into the body.

Food is moistened with saliva and chewed to form a ball of food.

c) Proteases digest proteins.

i) What do proteases break proteins down into? ....

ii) Why can't the gut absorb big molecules like fats and proteins?

....

Mixed Questions — B2 Topic 3

Q3 The diagram shows part of the **circulatory system**.

a) Name the blood vessels labelled W, X, Y and Z using the words in the box.

pulmonary vein   aorta
vena cava   pulmonary artery

W ....

X ....

Y ....

Z ....

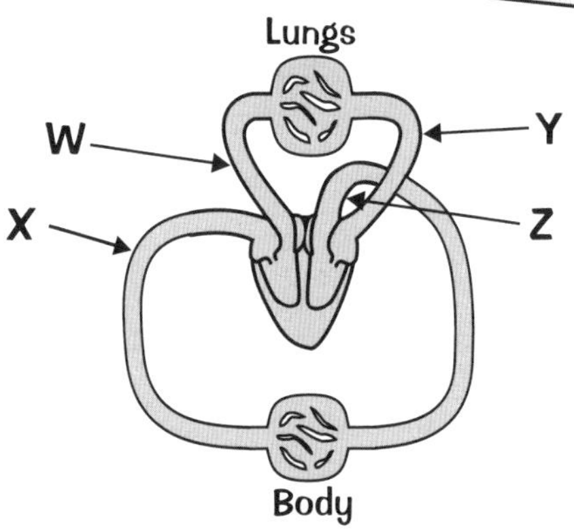

b) Which of the following statements is true?
Tick **one** box.

☐ Blood in the vena cava is deoxygenated, blood in the aorta is oxygenated.

☐ Blood in the aorta is deoxygenated, blood in the vena cava is oxygenated.

c) **i)** Which type of blood vessel contains valves? ....

ii) What is the function of these valves?

....

Q4 The **blood** is a huge **transport system**.

a) **i)** Circle the name of the blood cell shown on the right.

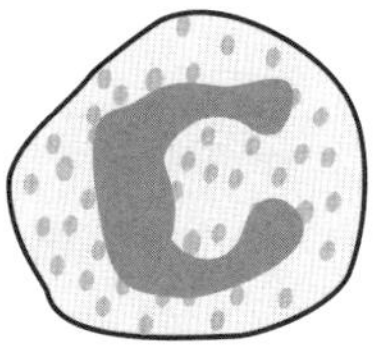

platelet   white blood cell   red blood cell

ii) Underline the function of this cell.

To defend the body against disease.   To help the blood clot at a wound.   To carry substances in the blood.

b) The cell on the right transports oxygen to all parts of the body.

i) Give **one** way in which this cell is adapted to perform its job.

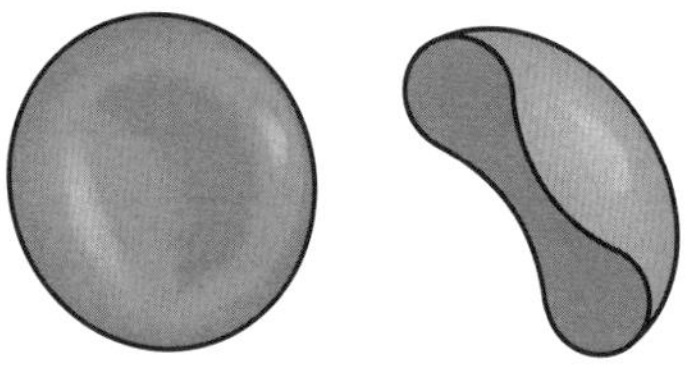

....

ii) Briefly explain how this adaptation allows it to do its job well.

....

....

....

Atoms

Q1   The diagram below shows the structure of a **helium atom**. Use the words in the box on the right to **label** the diagram.

| electron |
| proton |

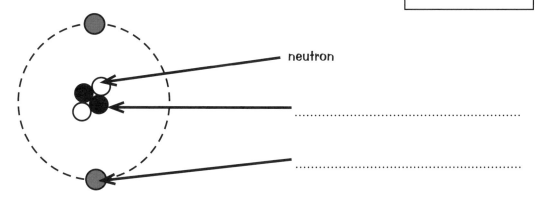

neutron

....

....

Q2   **Complete** this table.

Particle	Mass	Charge
	1	+1
Neutron	1	
Electron		−1

Q3   **Complete** the following sentences by filling in the gaps using the words below.

| electrons | atom | protons | zero |

a)   Atoms have a charge of ....

b)   An atom has the same number of .... and ....

c)   The nucleus is tiny compared to the overall size of the ....

Q4   What is it?

Choose from: **nucleus**   **electron**   **neutron**

a)   It's in the centre of the atom and contains protons and neutrons. ....

b)   It moves around the nucleus in shells. ....

c)   It's the lightest particle. ....

d)   It's heavy and has no charge. ....

Electron Shells

Q1   Tick the boxes to show whether each statement is **true** or **false**.

                                                                               True **False**

a)   Electrons move around the nucleus in energy levels called shells. ☐ ☐

b)   The outer shells are always filled first. ☐ ☐

c)   The second shell can take a maximum of eight electrons. ☐ ☐

d)   Atoms can't have more than two electrons in their third shell. ☐ ☐

e)   The first shell can take a maximum of eight electrons. ☐ ☐

Q2   Write down **two** things that are wrong with the **electrons** in this diagram.

1. ....

....

2. ....

....

Q3   Fill in the table with the **electronic configurations** for the following elements.
The first one has been done for you.

Element	Number of electrons	Electronic configuration
Beryllium	4	2.2
Oxygen	8	
Silicon	14	
Boron	5	
Aluminium	13	
Argon	18	

Electron Shells

Q4 **Chlorine** has 17 protons.

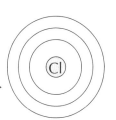

a) What is its electronic configuration? ....

b) Draw the electrons on the shells in the diagram.

c) How many energy levels are full in a chlorine atom?

....

Q5 Draw the **full electronic configurations** for these elements.
(The first three have been done for you.)

The number of protons each element has is shown in brackets after its name.

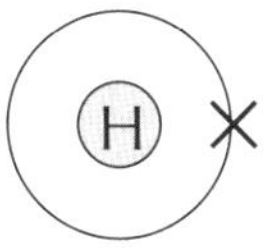

Hydrogen (1) 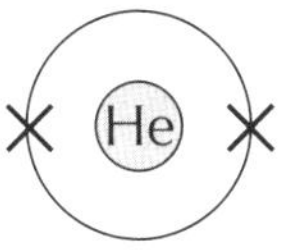   Helium (2) 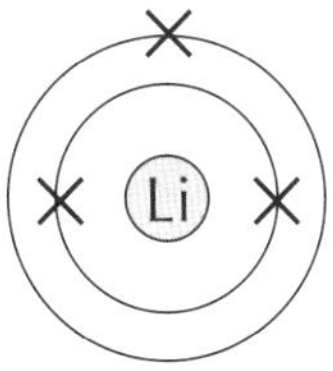   Lithium (3)

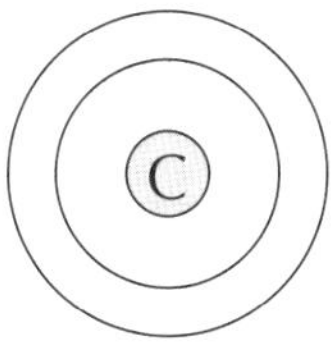

a) Carbon (6) 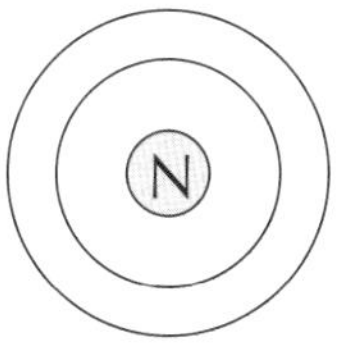   b) Nitrogen (7) 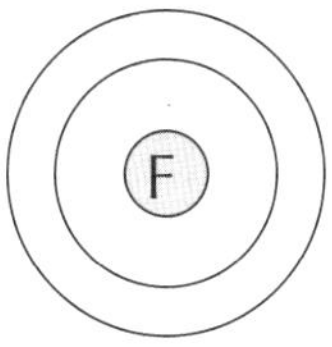   c) Fluorine (9)

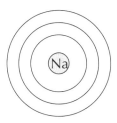 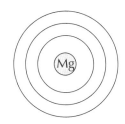

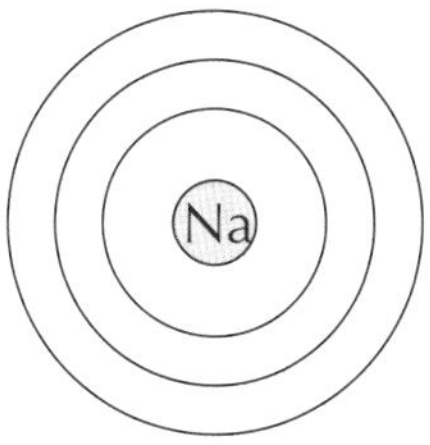

d) Sodium (11)   e) Magnesium (12) 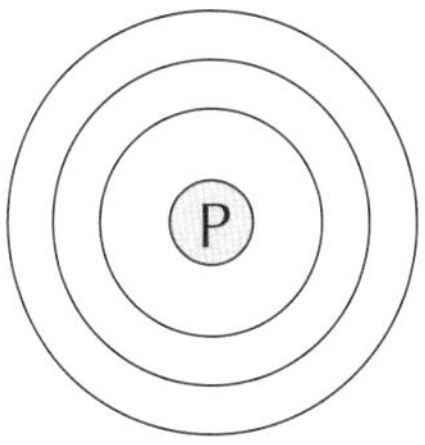   f) Phosphorus (15)

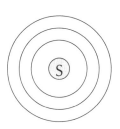 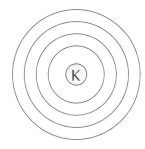 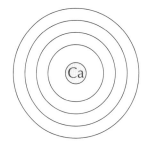

g) Sulfur (16)   h) Potassium (19)   i) Calcium (20)

Top Tips: Once you've learned the 'electron shell rules' these questions are pretty easy — as long as you know how many electrons go in each shell then all you have to do is pop them in. Sorted.

Elements and Numbers

Q1 Use the words below to fill in the gaps in this paragraph about **elements** and **atoms**.

mass	atomic	protons	atom

An element is a substance that is made up from only one type of ....

It's the number of .... in an atom that tells us what element it is.

The number of protons in an atom is called the .... number. The total

number of protons and neutrons in an atom is called the .... number.

Q2 Label the **atomic number** and **mass number** of magnesium on the diagram below.

a) .... ⟶ →24
b) .... ⟶ →12 Mg

Q3 Fill in the table below, using the periodic table (at the front of this book) to help you.

Element	Symbol	Mass Number	Number of Protons	Number of Electrons
Sodium	Na		11	
		16	8	8
Neon			10	10
	Ca			20

Q4 Sometimes there are **different forms** of the same element.

a) Circle the correct word(s) in each pair to complete the following sentences.

> Different forms of the same element have the same number of **neutrons / protons**
> but a different number of **neutrons / electrons**.
>
> This means they have different **mass numbers / atomic numbers**.

b) What is the **average mass** of the **different forms** of an element known as?

....

A Brief History of the Periodic Table

Q1 Mendeleev put all the **elements** he knew about in a **table**.

Complete the sentence below by circling the correct word(s) in the pair.

> Mendeleev organised his table based on the **colours** / **properties** of the elements and their compounds.

Q2 Tick the boxes to show whether the following statements about **Mendeleev** are **true** or **false**.

	True	False
a) Mendeleev was able to predict the properties of undiscovered elements.	☐	☐
b) Mendeleev put elements with similar properties in the same rows.	☐	☐

Q3 Mendeleev left gaps in his table. He then predicted the discovery of an element that would fill a gap in his Group 4, and called it '**ekasilicon**'.

a) Tick the correct box to explain why Mendeleev had to leave gaps in his table.

☐ He wanted to show compounds as well as elements in the table, so he left gaps to fill them in.

☐ He wanted the table to have the same number of elements on each side so he had to spread them out.

☐ He wanted to put elements with similar properties in the same columns. To make this work, he had to leave gaps.

b) The table below shows the **densities** of known elements in Mendeleev's Group 4.

'Ekasilicon' was eventually discovered and given another name. Use the table to decide which of the elements below is ekasilicon. Circle your choice.

palladium, 12.0 g/cm³   beryllium, 1.85 g/cm³

germanium, 5.32 g/cm³   copper, 8.92 g/cm³

Element	Density g/cm³
carbon	2.27
silicon	2.33
ekasilicon	
tin	7.31
lead	11.3

Top Tips: As new elements were discovered, Mendeleev's table grew to become the periodic table we still use today. That makes him a bit of a legend in the wonderful world of chemists.

The Periodic Table

Q1   Choose from the words in the box to fill in the blanks in the sentences below.

metals	group	non-metals	row

a)   A period in the periodic table is a .... of elements.

b)   Most of the elements in the periodic table are ....

c)   Metals and .... are found on opposite sides of the periodic table.

d)   Elements in the same .... have similar properties.

Q2   Tick the correct boxes to show whether the following statements are **true** or **false**.

		True	False
a)	Elements in a group have the same number of electrons in their outer shells.	☐	☐
b)	The periodic table shows the elements in order of decreasing atomic number along each row.	☐	☐
c)	The periodic table includes all the known compounds.	☐	☐

Q3   **Argon** is a very unreactive gas. Circle **two** elements below that you would expect to have **similar properties** to argon. Use a periodic table to help you.

calcium   helium   carbon   krypton   silicon   iodine

There's a periodic table on the inside of the front cover.

Q4   Use a **periodic table** to help you answer the following questions.

a)   Name one element in the same period as silicon. ....

b)   Name one element in the same group as potassium. ....

c)   Name one element that has 2 electrons in its outer shell. ....

Q5   **Fluorine** is a member of Group 7.

a)   How many electrons does a fluorine atom have in its outer shell? ....

b)   Explain why the only information you need to work this out is the group number.

....

Balancing Equations

Q1 State symbols give the **physical state** of a substance.

Give the **symbols** for the following states.

a) Solid   c) Gas

b) Liquid   d) Dissolved in water
                                 (aqueous)

Q2 Complete the following equations using the options in the box below.

a) $2Na + Cl_2 \rightarrow$ ....

b) $C_2H_6 + 3O_2 \rightarrow 2CO_2 +$ ....

$2NaCl$	$3H_2O$
	$2H_2$

c) $SnO_2 +$ .... $\rightarrow Sn + 2H_2O$

Q3 Here is an equation. It is **not** balanced correctly.

$$C + O_2 \rightarrow CO$$

Circle the **correctly balanced** version of this equation.

$$C + O_2 \rightarrow CO_2$$

$$C + O_2 \rightarrow 2CO$$

$$2C + O_2 \rightarrow 2CO$$

Q4 Karen has balanced these equations really quickly. She's got some of them wrong.
Tick the boxes to show whether the following equations are **balanced** correctly or incorrectly.

		Correctly balanced	Incorrectly balanced
a)	$H_2 + Cl_2 \rightarrow 2HCl$	☐	☐
b)	$CuO + HCl \rightarrow CuCl_2 + H_2O$	☐	☐
c)	$N_2 + H_2 \rightarrow NH_3$	☐	☐
d)	$CuO + H_2 \rightarrow Cu + H_2O$	☐	☐
e)	$CaCO_3 \rightarrow CaO + CO_2$	☐	☐

C2a Topic 1 — Atomic Structure and the Periodic Table

<u>Balancing Equations</u>

Q5 This is the **equation** for burning hydrogen in air.

$$2H_2 + O_2 \rightarrow 2H_2O$$

a) How many H and O atoms are shown on the **left-hand** side of the equation?

H ....2.... O ....2....

b) How many H and O atoms are shown on the **right-hand** side of the equation?

H ....2.... O ....2....

c) i) Is this equation balanced? ~~yes~~ No

ii) Explain your answer.

because their has to be same amount of oxygen as the start till the end.

Q6 Add **one** number to each of these equations so that they are **correctly balanced**.

a) $CuO + HBr \rightarrow CuBr_2 + H_2O_2$

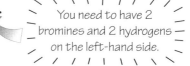
You need to have 2 bromines and 2 hydrogens on the left-hand side.

b) $H_2 + Br_2 \rightarrow HBr_2$

c) $Mg + O_2 \rightarrow 2MgO_2$

d) $2NaOH + H_2SO_4 \rightarrow Na_2SO_4 + H_2O_4$

e) $FeCl_2 + Cl_2 \rightarrow 2FeCl_3 + Cl_2$

$Fe_2O_3 + 3CO \rightarrow 2Fe + 3CO_2$

Q7 **Methane** (CH_4) can be burned in **oxygen** (O_2) to make **carbon dioxide** (CO_2) and **water** (H_2O).

a) Complete the **word equation** for this reaction.

methane + ...Oxygen.... → ....Carbon dioxide.... + ...water....

b) Write the **balanced symbol equation** for the reaction.

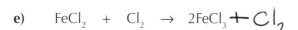

$CH_4 + O_2 \rightarrow CO_2 + H_2O$

Don't forget the oxygen ends up in both products.

$CO_2CH_4 + H_2O$

Top Tips: The most important thing to remember with balancing equations is that you can't change the **little numbers**. If you do that then you'll change the substance into something different — and you don't want that. Just take your time and work through everything bit by bit.

C2a Topic 1 — Atomic Structure and the Periodic Table

Ionic Bonding

Q1   Choose the correct words from the list below to complete the passage.

elements	ionic	ions	compounds

Atoms of different .... can form chemical bonds and join together

to create new ....   One way they can do this is by ....

bonding.   Electrons are transferred between atoms so they form ....

Q2   Tick **one** of the boxes below to show which statement is the best definition of an **ion**.

An ion is a compound that contains both positive and negative charges. ☐

An ion is a positively or negatively charged atom or group of atoms. ☐

An ion is a positively or negatively charged element. ☐

Q3   Tick the correct boxes to show whether the statements below are **true** or **false**.

                                                                          True   **False**

a)   In ionic bonding, ions lose or gain electrons to become atoms. ☐ ☐

b)   Ions with opposite charges attract each other. ☐ ☐

c)   Elements that lose electrons form positive ions. ☐ ☐

d)   Elements that gain electrons form cations. ☐ ☐

e)   Ions have full outer shells. ☐ ☐

Q4   Use the **diagram** to answer the following questions.

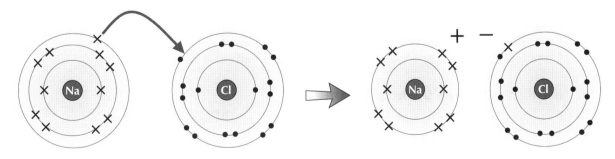

a)   Which group of the periodic table does **sodium** belong to? Circle the correct answer.

                            Group 1   **Group 7**

b)   Circle a number to show how many extra electrons **chlorine** needs to get a full outer shell.

                        7   **1**   **8**

Ionic Bonding

Q5   Draw lines to match each of the following **atoms** with the change
in the number of their electrons when they become **ions**.

Na	Lose 2
S	Lose 1
Be	Gain 2

Q6   Atoms can **gain** or **lose** electrons to get a full outer shell.

a)   Draw lines to match each of the following **ions** to their **charge**.

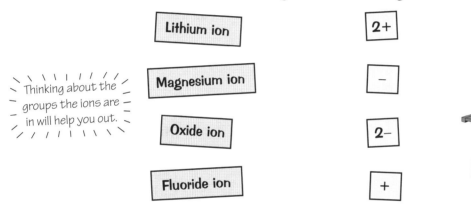

Lithium ion   2+

Thinking about the groups the ions are in will help you out.

Magnesium ion   −

Oxide ion   2−

Fluoride ion   +

b)   **i)** Which of the ions in part **a)** are **cations**? .... and ....

   ii) Which of the ions in part **a)** are **anions**? .... and ....

c)   What is formed when anions and cations **join** together?

   ....

Q7   An atom of **beryllium** has **two electrons** in its outer shell.
Complete the following sentences by circling the correct word(s) from each pair.

a)   Beryllium is in **Group 2** / **Group 6**.

b)   The charge on a beryllium ion will be **2+** / **2−**.

"Oi, give me that electron big nose!"

c)   A beryllium ion is **an anion** / **a cation**.

d)   It will form an ion by **gaining** / **losing** electrons.

e)   A beryllium ion can join with a **Group 1** / **Group 7** ion to make a compound.

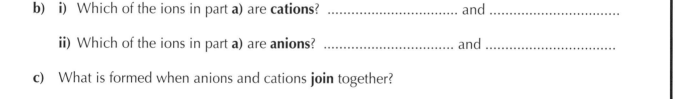

Ionic Compounds

Q1 Below is an incomplete 'dot and cross' diagram showing how
magnesium and **oxygen** react to give **magnesium oxide**.

a) **Circle** the electrons involved in the transfer and draw an **arrow**
to show the movement of electrons.

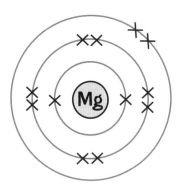 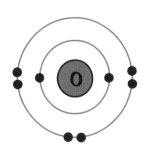

b) Write the **charge** of each of the ions formed in the reaction above.

Mg .... O ....

Q2 Mike carries out an experiment to find out if **magnesium oxide** conducts electricity.
He tests the compound when it's solid, when it's dissolved in water and when it's molten.

Complete the following table of results.

	Conducts electricity? (Yes / No)
When solid	
When dissolved in water	
When molten	

Q3 The melting point of **compound A** is **772 °C** and that of **compound B** is **−23 °C**.
Only one of the compounds is an ionic compound.

a) Which one is an ionic compound? ....

b) Explain your choice.

....

Naming Compounds and Finding Formulas

Q1   The names of compounds can tell us what **elements** they contain.

a) Use options from the box below to complete the passage about naming compounds.

oxygen	-IDE	-ATE	two

When .... elements join together the compound's name is

'something ....'.

When three or more different elements join together and one of them is ....

the compound's name is 'something ....'.

b) i) Circle the elements from the list below that make up potassium nitrate.

hydrogen   nitrogen   neon   potassium   oxygen

ii) Circle the elements from the list below that make up calcium carbonate.

oxygen   boron   calcium   carbon   hydrogen

Q2   Use information in the table to write out the **formulas** of the following compounds.

Positive Ions		**Negative Ions**	
Potassium	K^+	Chloride	Cl^-
Calcium	Ca^{2+}	Fluoride	F^-
Iron(II)	Fe^{2+}	Bromide	Br^-

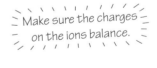
Make sure the charges on the ions balance.

a) potassium bromide   ....

b) iron(II) chloride   ....

c) calcium fluoride   ....

Q3   The formula of calcium nitrate is **Ca(NO$_3$)$_2$**.

The charge on the calcium ion is 2+. Give the charge on the nitrate ion. ....

Preparing Insoluble Salts

Q1   Some salts are **soluble** and some are **insoluble**.

Complete the following sentences by circling the correct word from each pair.

a)   Most chlorides, sulfates and nitrates are **soluble** / **insoluble** in water.

b)   Most hydroxides and carbonates are **soluble** / **insoluble** in water.

c)   Most sodium, potassium and ammonium salts are **soluble** / **insoluble** in water.

d)   Insoluble salts are made by **precipitation** / **electrolysis**.

Q2   **Lead nitrate** and **sodium sulfate** are two salts.

a)   State whether lead nitrate and sodium sulfate are soluble or insoluble.

Lead nitrate: ....

Sodium sulfate: ....

b)   Lead nitrate and sodium sulfate are reacted together.
Circle the **two** salts that are made in this reaction.

    sodium chloride   **lead sulfate**   **sodium nitrate**   **nitrogen sulfate**

c)   i)   Would a precipitate form during this reaction?

....

ii)   Explain your answer.

....

Q3   **Silver chloride** is an insoluble salt. It is made by reacting silver nitrate and sodium chloride.

a)   Put the **method** for preparing silver chloride in order by numbering the boxes (1-5) below.
One has been done for you.

☐ Scrape the silver chloride onto clean filter paper and leave to dry.

[1] In a test tube dissolve some silver nitrate in distilled water.
In another test tube dissolve some sodium chloride in distilled water.

☐ Tip the two solutions into a beaker and stir well until a precipitate forms.

☐ Rinse the solid with distilled water.

☐ Filter the contents of the beaker into a flask.

b)   Complete the word equation for the reaction.

.... + ... → silver chloride + ...

Barium Meal and Flame Tests

Q1   Choose from the words below to complete the passage about barium sulfate.

blood	toxic	insoluble	meal
blockages	gut	opaque	

Most barium salts are .... But barium sulfate is safe to

drink because it is .... This means it can't enter the

.... It just passes through the body. Barium sulfate is

.... to X-rays. When drunk it shows up the

.... in X-ray pictures. This means any problems,

e.g. .... , can be seen. Drinking barium sulfate before an

X-ray is known as a barium ....

Q2   Les had four samples of **metal compounds**. He carried out a flame test on each one.

a)   Describe how a flame test is done.

....

....

b)   Draw lines to match each coloured flame seen by Les to the metal ion that made it.

brick-red flame   Na⁺

yellow/orange flame   Cu²⁺

blue-green flame   K⁺

lilac flame   Ca²⁺

c)   Les wants to make a firework which will explode in his local football team's colour, **lilac**.
Which of the following compounds should he use? Circle your answer.

silver nitrate   sodium chloride   barium sulfate

potassium nitrate   calcium carbonate

Testing for Negative Ions and Spectroscopy

Q1 Choose from the words given to complete the passage below.

carbon dioxide	limewater	acid

Reacting a sample with dilute .... is a way of testing for carbonate ions.

If they are present then .... will be formed. You can test for this by

bubbling it through .... to see if it becomes milky.

Q2 Answer the following questions on testing for **sulfate** ions.

a) Which **two** chemicals are used to test for sulfate ions? Circle the correct answers.

dilute hydrochloric acid   limewater   barium chloride   sulfuric acid

b) What would you **see** after adding these chemicals to a sulfate compound?

....

Q3 Deirdre wants to find out if a solution contains **chloride** ions.
Tick the correct box to show how she could do this.

You're being a bit negative today, aren't you?

No...

☐ Add dilute nitric acid.
Then add silver nitrate solution.
Look for a white precipitate.

☐ Add dilute hydrochloric acid.
Then add silver nitrate solution.
Look for a white precipitate.

☐ Add dilute hydrochloric acid.
Then add silver nitrate solution.
Look for a grey precipitate.

☐ Add dilute hydrochloric acid.
Then add barium chloride solution.
Look for a white precipitate.

Q4 Spectroscopy can be used to **identify** elements.

a) Circle **two** elements from the list below that were **discovered** using spectroscopy.

caesium   sodium   oxygen   rubidium

b) Give **one** advantage of using spectroscopy to identify elements.

....

Covalent Bonding

Q1 Tick the boxes to show whether each statement is **true** or **false**.

True False

a) Covalent bonding involves sharing a pair of electrons between two atoms. ☐ ☐

b) Atoms make covalent bonds to get a full outer shell of electrons. ☐ ☐

c) When atoms make covalent bonds they form molecules. ☐ ☐

d) Hydrogen can form two covalent bonds. ☐ ☐

e) Carbon can form four covalent bonds. ☐ ☐

Q2 Complete the following table to show how many electrons are needed to **fill up** the **outer shell** of these atoms.

Atom	Carbon	Chlorine	Hydrogen	Nitrogen	Oxygen
Electronic Configuration	2.4	2.8.7	1	2.5	2.6
Number of electrons needed to fill outer shell					

Q3 Complete the following diagrams by adding the **electrons**. Only the outer shells are shown.

a) Hydrogen chloride (HCl)

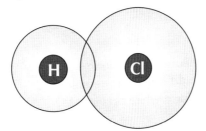

c) Methane (CH$_4$)

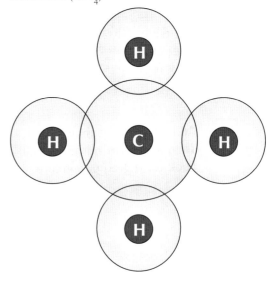

b) Water (H$_2$O)

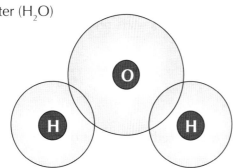

Top Tips: Don't get covalent bonding muddled up with ionic bonding — there's a big difference between atoms sharing electrons and atoms giving and taking electrons.

Covalent Substances — Two Kinds

Q1 Fill in the blanks in the following paragraph by choosing words from the list.

weak	small	easy	strong

Simple molecular covalent substances have ....

molecules with .... covalent bonds. The molecules have

.... forces between them. Because of this it is fairly

.... to separate the molecules from each other.

Q2 Complete the following sentences by circling the correct word in each pair.
Explain your answers below.

a) The melting and boiling points of simple molecular covalent substances are **low / high**

because ....

b) Simple molecular covalent substances **do / don't** conduct electricity

because ....

Q3 Circle the correct words in each pair to complete the sentences below.

All the **atoms / ions** in giant molecular covalent structures are bonded to each other by
strong / weak covalent bonds. This means that they have **low / high** melting points.

Q4 There are two types of **covalent** substance.

a) For each of the substances below, say whether it's **simple molecular** or **giant molecular**.
Write your answers on the dotted line below each substance.

Graphite	Diamond	Hydrogen

....

....

b) Which of the three substances above would **conduct electricity**?

....

Classifying Elements and Compounds

Q1 Complete the following table by placing a **tick** or a **cross** in each box.

One has been
done for you.

Property	Ionic	Giant Molecular	Simple Molecular
High melting and boiling points			
Can conduct electricity when solid		**X** except graphite	
Can conduct electricity when melted		 except graphite	

Q2 The **properties** of three substances are given below.

Substance	Melting Point (°C)	Good Electrical Conductor?
A	2000	Only when melted or dissolved
B	2500	No
C	20	No

Identify the **structure** of each substance. Use the words from the list below. Give a reason for your choice.

Only use each
option once.

giant molecular	ionic	simple molecular

a) Substance A: ....

Reason: ....

....

b) Substance B: ....

Reason: ....

....

c) Substance C: ....

Reason: ....

....

Top Tips: You need to be able to work out whether a substance has an ionic, giant molecular or simple molecular structure. The clues are boiling point, melting point and electrical conductivity.

Separation Techniques

Q1 Some liquid mixtures are **immiscible** and some are **miscible**.

a) Draw lines to match each of the sentences below to the correct type of mixture.

Separates out into layers when allowed to stand

Miscible

Can be separated by fractional distillation

Doesn't separate out into layers when allowed to stand

Immiscible

Can be separated with a separating funnel

b) Bill wants to separate a mixture of two liquids using a **separating funnel**.
Put the numbers 1-3 in the boxes below to show how he should do this.

☐ Open the tap to drain off the lower layer into a beaker.

☐ Let the mixture stand so it separates out into layers.

☐ Put the mixture in a separating funnel with a tap.

Q2 Liquid air can be separated using **fractional distillation**.

a) Complete the sentences below by circling the correct word in each pair.

The mixture is **heated / cooled** so that the liquid air becomes gases.

The gases rise up the **beaker / column** and cool down.

When the gases cool down enough they will **condense / evaporate**.

But the different liquids will do this at different **temperatures / pressures**.

They can then be collected **together / separately**.

b) Name **two gases** that are produced when air is separated by fractional distillation.

1. ....

2. ....

Chromatography

Q1 Ella has received a horrible letter from someone and there are **three suspects**. She is going to compare the ink on the letter with the printer inks used by the three suspects.

a) Number the boxes 1 to 3 to put the method Ella will use in order.

☐ Put the filter paper in a beaker so the bottom is dipped in solvent.

☐ Compare the pattern from the letter ink with the patterns from the printer inks to find out which one it came from.

☐ Draw a line in pencil near the bottom of some filter paper. Put spots of each ink being tested on it.

b) Circle the correct word(s) in each pair to complete the passage below about paper chromatography.

> The **solvent** / **current** seeps up the paper taking the samples of inks with it.
>
> The different chemicals in the inks travel at **the same** / **different** speeds .
>
> So they form spots in **the same** / **different** places.

c) The results Ella gets when she analyses the ink from the letter and the ink from the three printers are on the right. Which suspect(s) can she **leave out** of the investigation?

....

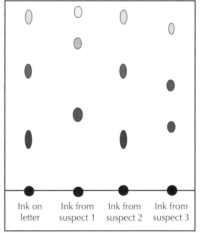

Ink on letter | Ink from suspect 1 | Ink from suspect 2 | Ink from suspect 3

Q2 A **food colouring** was analysed using **paper chromatography**. The chromatogram shown on the right was produced.

Use the formula to work out the R_f value of each dye.

$$R_f = \frac{\text{distance travelled by substance}}{\text{distance travelled by solvent}}$$

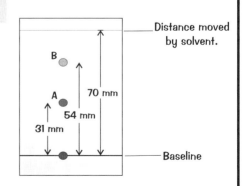

Distance moved by solvent.

B
A
70 mm
54 mm
31 mm
Baseline

a) Dye A ....

b) Dye B ....

<u>Mixed Questions — C2a Topics 1, 2 & 3</u>

Q1 Answer the following questions about the **periodic table**.

a) If an element is in Group 1, how many electrons will it have in its outer electron shell? ....

b) An ion of an element has a 2+ charge. Which group is the element **most likely** to be in? ....

c) If an ion has a 1– charge, then which group is it **most likely** to be in? ....

d) Complete this table by filling in the **electronic configurations** of the elements. Two have been done for you.

The number of protons is shown in brackets after each element.

Group 1	Group 2	Group 3	Group 7	Group 0
Lithium (3)	Beryllium (4) 2.2	Boron (5)	Fluorine (9)	Neon (10)
Sodium (11)	Magnesium (12)	Aluminium (13)	Chlorine (17)	Argon (18) 2.8.8

e) Hydrogen atoms can only make **one covalent bond**. Circle the number of hydrogen atoms a **chlorine** atom will bond with to give it a full outer shell of electrons.

7   1   2   *Use your answer to d) to help you.*

Q2 **Calcium** is in **Group 2** of the periodic table.

a) i) Based on its position in the periodic table, circle an element from the list below which has **similar properties** to calcium.

  bromine   oxygen   magnesium

ii) Explain your answer.

....

b) Calcium reacts with **chlorine** to form calcium chloride.

i) Write the **word equation** for this reaction.

....

ii) The charge on the chloride ion is **1–**. Work out the **formula** of calcium chloride.

....

iii) Write a **balanced symbol equation** for the reaction.

....

Mixed Questions — C2a Topics 1, 2 & 3

Q3 Stanley is trying to **identify** a mystery substance.

He puts a sample of the substance in a Bunsen flame.

a) Circle the result you would expect Stanley to see if the mystery compound contained Ca^{2+} ions.

| brick-red flame | yellow/orange flame | lilac flame |

...and add a splash of $CaSO_4$, with a dollop of $MgBr_2$ and a dash of Worcester sauce...

b) In fact, he sees a blue-green flame. This means Stanley's compound doesn't contain any Ca^{2+} ions. What type of ion does it contain?

....

c) Stanley thinks that his compound could be a sulfate.

i) Sulfates contain SO_4^{2-} ions. Are these cations or anions?

....

ii) Describe a test he could do to see if the compound is a sulfate.

....

....

Q4 **Fluorine** is in **Group 7** of the periodic table and **lithium** is in **Group 1**. Their electronic configurations are shown below.

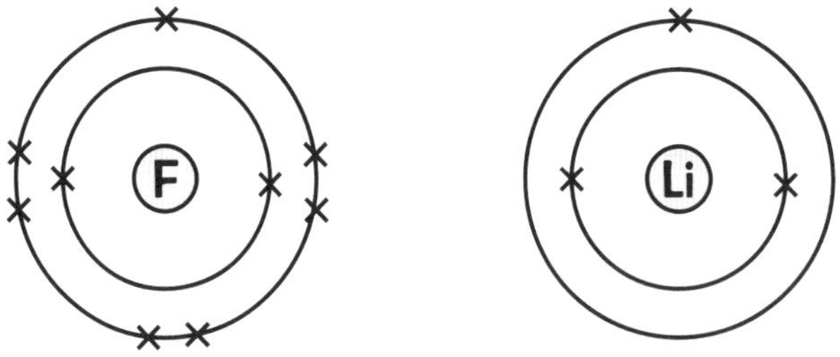

a) Lithium and fluorine react to make lithium fluoride. Work out the formula of lithium fluoride.

....

b) i) Lithium chloride conducts electricity when melted but not when solid. What type of **bonding** is involved in this compound?

....

ii) Circle the most likely **melting point** for lithium chloride.

605 °C   10 °C   0 °C   22 °C

Properties of Metals

Q1 A new element has been found on Mars. Scientists test the element to work out if it's a **metal**. Circle **two properties** in the list below that are common to **metals**.

sets on fire easily   conduct electricity

malleable

breaks easily   dissolve in water

Q2 A group of **metals** is found in the **central section** of the periodic table.

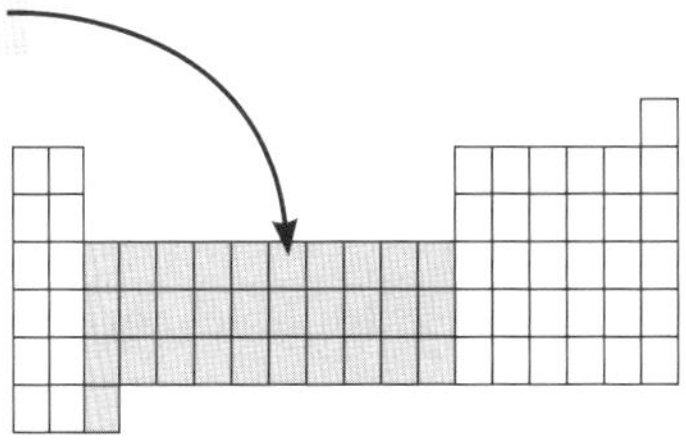

a) What name is given to this group of metals?

....

b) Complete the sentence below by circling the correct word in the pair.

The metals in this group have **high** / **low** melting points.

c) What are the properties of compounds formed by these metals? Tick **one** box in the list below.

they have low melting points ☐   they are colourful ☐

they are liquids ☐   they are inert ☐

Q3 All metals have a similar **structure**. This is why many metals have similar **properties**.

a) The diagram below shows the structure of a metal. Use the words given to label parts **A** and **B**.

| electron | | positive ion |

A ....

B ....

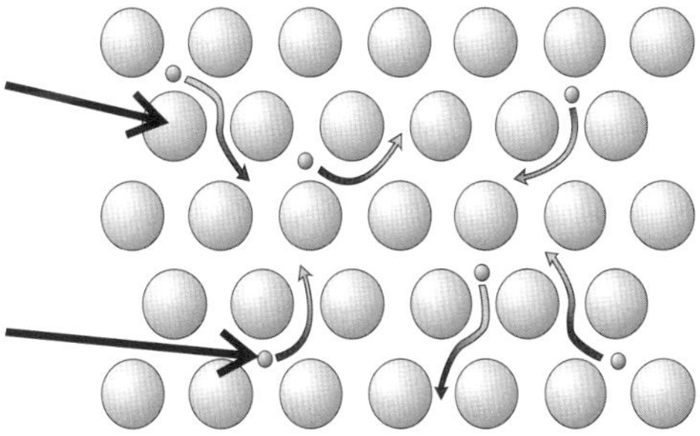

b) What is unusual about the electrons in a metal? Circle the correct answer.

    A They have a positive charge.   **B** They are arranged in a regular pattern.

    C They are delocalised.   **D** They have no charge.

Top Tips: Remember, most elements are metals and most metals have similar structures and properties. But they're not all the same — like people, metals are all a little bit different.

Group 1 — The Alkali Metals

Q1 Circle the correct chemical symbol for each **alkali metal** below.

a) | lithium | | Li | | Lm | | L |

b) | sodium | | S | | Na | | K |

c) | potassium | | P | | K | | Pt |

Q2 **Sodium**, **potassium** and **lithium** are all alkali metals.

a) Circle the diagram below which shows where the alkali metals are found in the periodic table.

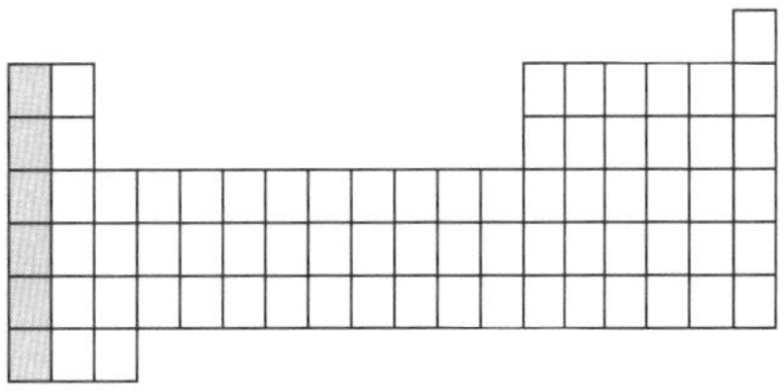

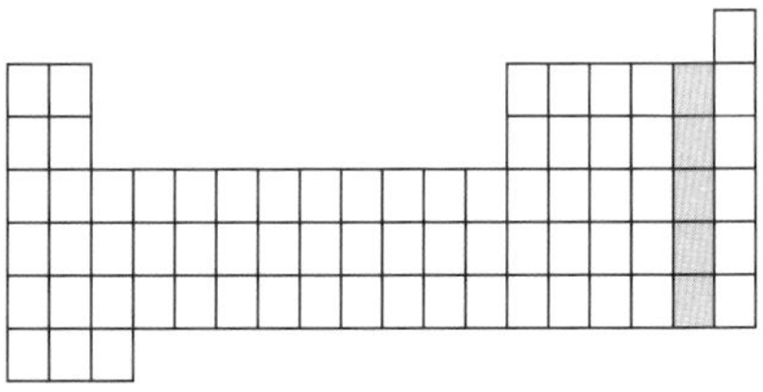

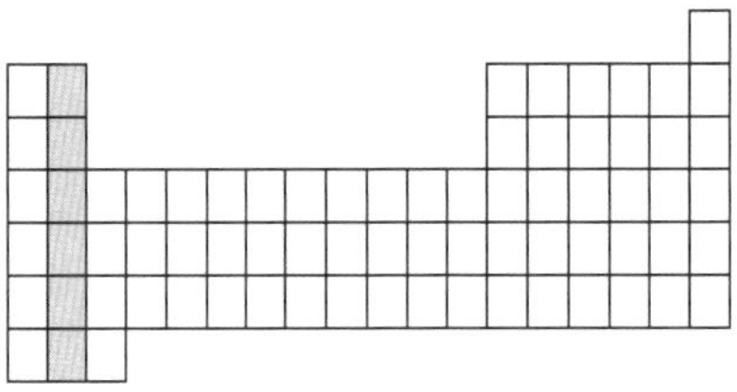

b) Circle **two** properties of alkali metals in the list below.

do not react   hard   low boiling points

low melting points   do not conduct electricity   soft

Q3 Raj has given Donna a present — some **lithium**. She drops it into a glass of water by mistake.

a) Circle the word in the list below that describes the solution formed at the end of the reaction.

acidic   neutral   alkaline

b) Donna says:
"Lithium reacts with water to make lithium chloride and carbon dioxide."
Raj says that Donna is wrong. Write out a corrected version of Donna's statement below.

....

....

Group 1 — The Alkali Metals

Q4 Three different **alkali metals**, A, B and C, were dropped into bowls of water.
The time taken for each metal to **disappear** was written down and is shown in the table.

a) i) Which of these is the most reactive metal?
Circle the correct answer.

Metal A   Metal C
          Metal B

METAL	TIME TAKEN TO DISAPPEAR (s)
A	27
B	8
C	42

ii) Explain how you can tell.

....

....

b) Describe how the reactivity of the alkali metals changes down Group 1 of the periodic table.

....

c) The three metals used were lithium, sodium and potassium.
Use the results in the table to match them up to the correct metals A, B and C.

Metal A   Metal B   Metal C

Lithium is at the top of Group 1. Then comes sodium, and then comes potassium.

potassium   lithium   sodium

Q5 Rubidium is **further down** Group 1 than lithium, sodium and potassium.

a) Tick **two** boxes to show which of the following statements are true.

☐ Rubidium is less reactive than potassium.

☐ Rubidium is more reactive than lithium.

☐ Sodium will take longer to completely react with water than rubidium.

b) Caesium and francium are also alkali metals. Look at the periodic table.
Which of the two metals would you expect to be **more reactive**?

There's a periodic table on the inside of the front cover.

....

c) Explain your answer to part **b)**.

....

....

Top Tips: Make sure that you know these alkali metals inside out before the exam.
You need to know where they are in the periodic table, and what goes on in their reactions with water.
Make sure you know about how their reactivity changes as you go down the group as well.

<u>Group 7 — The Halogens</u>

Q1   Circle the letter (A, B or C) that shows where the **halogens** are found in the periodic table.

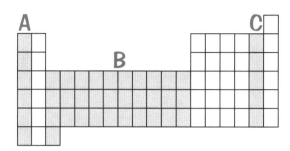

Q2   Draw lines to match the halogens to their **descriptions** and **reactivity**.

HALOGEN	DESCRIPTION	REACTIVITY
bromine	green gas	most reactive
chlorine	grey solid	least reactive
iodine	orange liquid	quite reactive

Q3   Tick the correct boxes to say whether these statements are **true** or **false**.

                                                                                        True   False

a)   Bromine is very unreactive.

b)   Potassium chloride is a metal halide.

c)   The halogens become less reactive as you go down the group.

d)   Chlorine gas is made up of molecules which each contain three chlorine atoms.

e)   Fluorine is the most reactive halogen.

Q4   Halogens react with hydrogen to form **hydrogen halides**.

a)   State the name of the compound formed when chlorine reacts with hydrogen.

     ....

b)   The product of the reaction between chlorine and hydrogen is dissolved in water.
     Is the solution acidic or alkaline?

     ....

Group 7 — The Halogens

Q5 Halogens can react with **metals** to form salts.

a) What is the name given to the salts formed by the reaction of a halogen with a metal?
Circle the correct answer below.

hydrogen halides   acids   alkalis

         halogen metals   metal halides

b) Fill in the blanks in the following equations using the words or symbols from the box below.

magnesium fluoride $AlBr_3$ iodine   aluminium F_2

i) .... + bromine → aluminium bromide

ii) $2Al + 3Br_2 →$ 2............

iii) Potassium + ... → potassium iodide

iv) Magnesium + fluorine → ....

v) $Mg +$ .... → MgF_2

Q6 Scott does an experiment to see what happens when a **halogen** reacts with a solution containing **halide ions**. He adds the halogen to the halide solution to see if a reaction takes place.

a) What is the **name** given to a reaction where one halogen takes the place of another in a solution?

....

b) Complete the table to show if a reaction took place when the halogen was added to each solution.

Solution	Halogen added to solution	Reaction (yes or no)
potassium fluoride	bromine	no
potassium chloride	iodine	
potassium bromide	chlorine	
potassium iodide	bromine	

Remember — a more reactive halogen will push out a less reactive halogen from a solution.

c) Explain why there was no reaction when bromine was added to potassium fluoride solution.

....

....

....

Group 0 — The Noble Gases

Q1   Where are the noble gases located in the periodic table?

....

Q2   **Helium** and **argon** are noble gases which are used in **industry**.

a)   Complete the table using the numbers provided to show the **densities** of helium and argon.

| 0.0018 |

Element	Density (g/cm³)
Helium	
Neon	0.0009
Argon	

| 0.0002 |

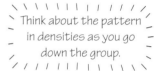
Think about the pattern in densities as you go down the group.

b)   Draw lines to match helium and argon to their uses.

balloons   argon   airships

light bulbs   helium   protects metals that are being welded

Q3   The noble gases were **discovered** long after many of the other elements.

a)   Why did it take scientists so long to discover the noble gases?

....

....

b)   Circle the correct word(s) in each pair to complete the passage below.

> The noble gases were discovered when scientists noticed that the density of nitrogen
>
> made in **chemical reactions / fractional distillation** was different to the density of nitrogen
>
> taken from **water / air**. The scientists suggested that the nitrogen from the **water / air**
>
> must have other **metals / gases** mixed in with it.

Top Tips: The examiners will expect you to know quite a bit about certain groups in the
periodic table — the halogens, the alkali metals, the noble gases and the transition metals. Make sure
you're clear on their general properties and how these change as you move down or up each group.

Energy Transfer in Reactions

Q1 Look at the following reaction.

$$\textbf{A}\,\textbf{B} + \textbf{C} \longrightarrow \textbf{A}\,\textbf{C} + \textbf{B}$$

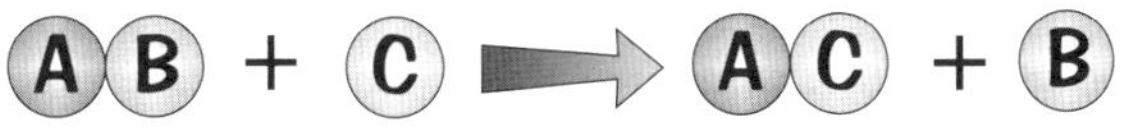

a) From the options below, tick the correct box to show which bond is broken during the reaction.

☐ A — B   ☐ A — C   ☐ B — C

b) **i)** Is **bond breaking** exothermic or endothermic? ....

   ii) Explain your answer to part **i)**.

   ....

Q2 Use the words from the box to fill in the gaps in the paragraph below.

formed	endothermic	broken	collide	particles	exothermic

A chemical reaction takes place when .... in the reactants
.... When this happens, old bonds may be ....
and new bonds may be .... Bond breaking is an
.... process and bond formation is an .... process.

Q3 Chemical reactions may be **exothermic** or **endothermic**.

a) Circle the correct words in this paragraph about **exothermic** reactions.

Exothermic reactions **take in / give out** energy overall, in the form of **heat / sound**.
This is shown by a **fall / rise** in **temperature / mass**.

b) Tick the correct boxes to show whether the following reactions are exothermic or endothermic.

	Exothermic	Endothermic
i) Photosynthesis	☐	☐
ii) Combustion	☐	☐
iii) An explosion	☐	☐
iv) Dissolving ammonium nitrate in water	☐	☐

Energy Transfer in Reactions

Q4 Describe what an **endothermic** reaction is.

....

....

Q5 The equation for the reaction between **methane** and **oxygen** is shown below.

methane + oxygen ⟶ carbon dioxide + water

a) Is energy taken in or given out when the bonds in the methane and oxygen molecules break?

....

b) Is energy taken in or given out when the bonds in the carbon dioxide and water molecules form?

....

c) Methane is a fuel often used in cooking and heating. Do you think that burning methane is an exothermic or an endothermic process? Explain your answer.

....

....

d) Which of the following statements about burning methane is true? Circle **one** letter.

A   The energy needed to break bonds is greater than the energy given out forming bonds.

B   The energy needed to break bonds is less than the energy given out forming bonds.

C   The energy needed to break bonds is the same as the energy given out forming bonds.

Q6 Here are some practical uses of chemical reactions. In the spaces below, state whether each reaction is **endothermic** or **exothermic**.

a) A camping stove burns gas to heat a pan of beans.   ....

b) Chemical cool packs are used by athletes to treat injuries.
They are put on the skin and draw heat away from the injury.   ....

c) Self-heating cans of coffee contain chemicals in the base. When the chemicals are mixed together they produce heat which warms the can.   ....

d) Coal is burnt in a power station to heat water and produce electricity.   ....

Energy Changes and Measuring Temperature

Q1 Fiz is cold. To take her mind off it, she decides to find out the **temperature change** during a reaction. The equipment Fiz used for the experiment is shown below.

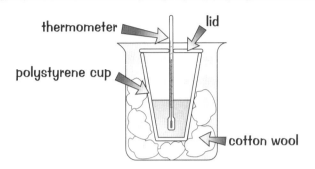

a) Explain why Fiz should measure the temperature of the reactants **before starting** the reaction.

....

b) State the purpose of the **lid** and **cotton wool** used in the experiment.

....

....

c) Why is it difficult to get **an accurate result** for the temperature change in an experiment like this?

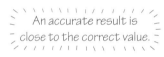
An accurate result is close to the correct value.

....

Q2 Rashid mixed sodium hydroxide solution with dilute hydrochloric acid. He recorded the **temperature** of the reaction mixture every **5** seconds for the first 30 seconds of the reaction. The graph below shows his results.

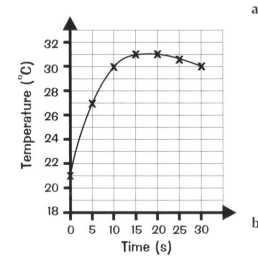

a) **i)** What was the highest temperature reached during the reaction?

....

ii) Using your answer to part **i)**, work out the maximum change in temperature during the reaction.

....

....

b) Circle the **two** words below that correctly describe the reaction in this experiment.

neutralisation   displacement

endothermic   precipitation   exothermic

Rates of Reaction

Q1   Tick the correct boxes to say whether these statements are **true** or **false**.

                                                                                       True   False

a)   The rate of a reaction is the speed of the chemical reaction.   ☐   ☐

b)   The rate of a reaction is the amount of product a chemical reaction makes.   ☐   ☐

c)   Reactions can be very fast, very slow, or somewhere in between.   ☐   ☐

d)   There are only three factors that affect the rate of a reaction.   ☐   ☐

Q2   Circle the correct word(s) in each pair to complete the statements below about **rates of reaction**.

a)   The **higher** / **lower** the temperature, the faster the rate of a reaction.

b)   A **higher** / **lower** concentration will reduce the rate of a reaction.

c)   A smaller surface area of a solid reactant **increases** / **decreases** the rate of a reaction.

d)   A catalyst **does** / **does not** affect the rate of a reaction.

Q3   Marble chips with **different surface areas** were reacted with hydrochloric acid. The **same mass** of marble was used each time. The graph below shows the amount of **gas** given off when using large marble chips (X), medium marble chips (Y) and small marble chips (Z).

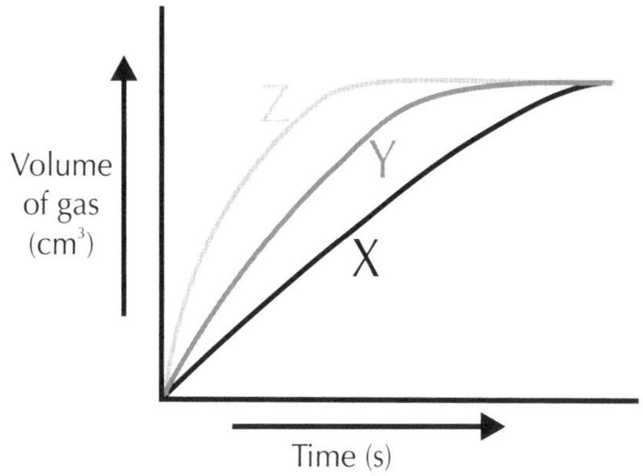

a)   i)   Which curve (X, Y or Z) shows the **fastest** reaction? Circle the correct answer.

                            X   **Y**   **Z**

     ii) How can you tell this by looking at the graph?

     ....

     ....

     ....

Volume of gas (cm³) vs *Time (s)* graph showing curves Z, Y, and X.

b)   Explain why the three lines become **flat** as the reaction continues.

....

c)   'Reaction Z using small marble chips produced a larger volume of gas than reactions X and Y.'
Is this statement correct? Explain your answer.

....

....

Rates of Reaction Experiments

Q1   Circle the correct word in each pair below to complete the paragraph.

> When you crush up a large solid into powder, you **increase / decrease**
>
> its surface area. This means it reacts **slower / faster**. Large lumps have
>
> a smaller **surface area / concentration**, so they react more **slowly / quickly**.

Q2   Matilda did an experiment to look at the effect of **surface area** on the rate of a reaction. She added dilute hydrochloric acid to **large marble chips** and measured the volume of gas given off during the reaction. She did the experiment again using the same mass of **powdered marble**.

   a) Circle one piece of equipment in the list below that Matilda would need to do the experiment.

   thermometer   catalyst   stopwatch   Bunsen burner

   b) The graph below shows Matilda's results. Which curve, **A** or **B**, shows the reaction where **large pieces** of marble were used?

   ....

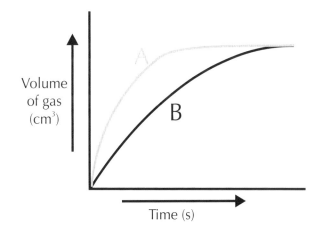

   c) On the graph above, draw the curve you would get if you used the **same mass** of **medium** sized marble pieces. Label it C.

   d) Balance the symbol equation for this reaction:

   $CaCO_3 + \quad HCl \rightarrow \quad CaCl_2 + \quad CO_2 + \quad H_2O$

   e) Give **one** factor which Matilda must keep the same each time she does this experiment.

   ....

Rates of Reaction Experiments

Q3   There isn't much on TV, so Yasmin decides to look at the effect of **temperature** on the rate of the reaction between marble chips and hydrochloric acid.

This graph shows her results:

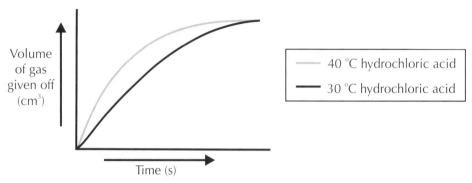

a)   As the temperature increases, does the reaction get **faster** or **slower**? ....

b)   Yasmin repeats the experiment using 50 °C acid and the same mass of marble chips. Sketch the line for this onto the graph above.

Q4   Sam reacted marble chips with **highly concentrated** hydrochloric acid. He measured the loss in mass of the reactants during the reaction.

Sam plotted his results onto the graph below.

a)   Sam did the reaction again using a **low concentration** of acid. Using the data in the table below, plot a second line onto the graph.

Time (s)	Average loss in mass (g)
5	1.0
10	1.7
15	2.5
20	3.1
25	3.5
30	3.5

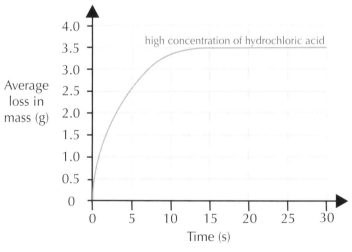

b)   Circle **one** letter to show the **conclusion** that you might draw from this graph.

    A   Rate of reaction depends on the temperature of the reactants.

    B   Increasing the concentration of the acid has no effect on the rate of reaction.

    C   Rate of reaction depends on the acid concentration.

    D   Rate of reaction depends on the mass of the marble chips.

Catalysts

Q1 Tick the correct boxes to say whether these statements are **true** or **false**.

	True	False
a) A catalyst can be used over and over again.	☐	☐
b) A catalyst speeds up the rate of a chemical reaction.	☐	☐
c) Catalysts are used up in a chemical reaction.	☐	☐
d) Using a catalyst in a reaction makes more product than not using a catalyst.	☐	☐

Q2 a) Use the words from the box to fill in the gaps in the paragraph below.

dioxide	fuel	catalysts	water	monoxide	oxygen

One use of .... is in catalytic converters in car exhausts.

The exhaust can give off poisonous gases like carbon .... if petrol

doesn't burn properly. The catalytic converter increases the rate at which unburnt

.... in exhaust gases reacts with .... in the air.

The reaction makes carbon .... and ....

b) Tick the box next to **two** features of catalytic converters that make them useful in this role.

☐ They have a large surface area.   ☐ They have a high concentration of catalyst.

☐ They react with oxygen.   ☐ They work best at high temperatures.

Q3 Mary uses a chemical reaction to produce a **gas**. She tries three different catalysts (**R**, **S** and **T**) to see how they affect the rate of the reaction.

a) The graph of Mary's results is shown on the right.
Using the graph, decide which curve (**R**, **S**, or **T**)
shows the best catalyst to use. Circle the correct letter below.

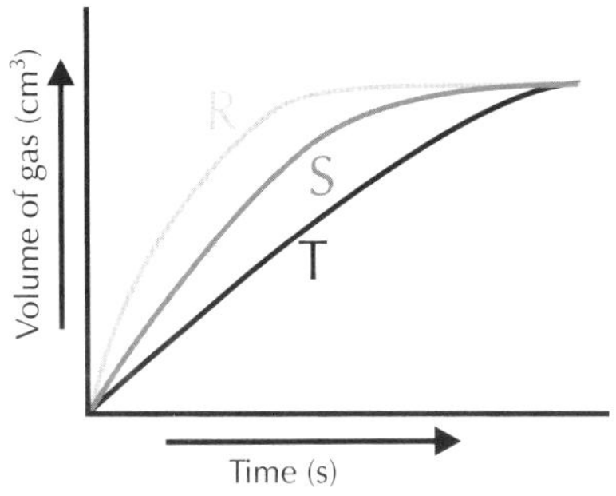

R   S   T

b) Explain your answer.

....

....

Relative Formula Mass

Q1 a) Explain how the **relative formula mass** of a **compound** is calculated.

....

b) Work out the **relative formula mass (M_r)** for each of the following:

> A_r is short for 'relative atomic mass'.

i) water, H_2O. (A_r of H = 1, A_r of O = 16)

....

ii) calcium chloride, $CaCl_2$. (A_r of Ca = 40, A_r of Cl = 35.5)

....

iii) potassium hydroxide, KOH. (A_r of K = 39, A_r of O = 16, A_r of H = 1)

....

iv) nitric acid, HNO_3. (A_r of H = 1, A_r of N = 14, A_r of O = 16)

....

v) sulfuric acid, H_2SO_4. (A_r of H = 1, A_r of S = 32, A_r of O = 16)

....

vi) ammonium nitrate, NH_4NO_3. (A_r of N = 14, A_r of H = 1, A_r of O = 16)

....

Q2 The relative formula mass of **sodium nitrate** ($NaNO_3$) is **85**. What is the relative atomic mass (A_r) of sodium? (A_r of nitrogen = 14, A_r of oxygen = 16)

....

....

....

Top Tips: The periodic table really comes in useful here. You'll probably be given the relative atomic masses for the elements in the question but if not, you can find them in the periodic table. That's pretty lucky because (unless you're Einstein) there's no way you could learn them all.

Percentage Composition by Mass

Q1   The **formula** for calculating the **percentage mass** of an element in a compound is shown below.

$$\text{Percentage mass of an element in a compound} = \frac{A_r \times \text{No. of atoms (of that element)}}{M_r \text{ (of whole compound)}} \times 100$$

a)   Calculate the relative molecular mass (M_r) of **ammonium nitrate**, NH_4NO_3.
(A_r of N = 14, A_r of H = 1, A_r of O = 16)

....

b)   Calculate the **percentage mass** of the following elements in ammonium nitrate.

i) Nitrogen ....

ii) Hydrogen ....

iii) Oxygen ....

Q2   **Nitrogen monoxide**, NO, reacts with oxygen, O_2, to form **nitrogen dioxide** (NO_2).

a)   Calculate the percentage mass of **nitrogen** in **nitrogen monoxide**. (A_r of N = 14, A_r of O = 16)
Give your answer to one decimal place.

....

b)   Calculate the percentage mass of **oxygen** in **nitrogen dioxide**. (A_r of N = 14, A_r of O = 16)
Give your answer to one decimal place.

....

Q3 a)   Calculate the percentage mass of **oxygen** in each of the following compounds.
Give your answers to one decimal place.

i) Fe_2O_3 (A_r of Fe = 56, A_r of O = 16)

....

ii) H_2O (A_r of H = 1, A_r of O = 16)

....

iii) $CaCO_3$ (A_r of Ca = 40, A_r of C = 12, A_r of O = 16)

....

b)   Which compound has the **greatest** percentage mass of oxygen?

....

Empirical Formulas

Q1 a) State what is meant by the **empirical formula** of a compound.

....

b) **30.8 g** of **nitrogen** and **70.4 g** of **oxygen** react together.
Use the table below to work out the empirical formula of the compound formed.
The first row has been filled in for you.
(A_r of N = 14, A_r of O = 16)

	N	O
1. Write in the reacting masses.	30.8 g	70.4 g
2. Divide the reacting masses by the A_r for each element.		
3. Are the numbers whole numbers? If not, turn them into a whole number ratio.		
4. Find the simplest ratio.	:	
5. State the empirical formula.		

Try multiplying by 10 to get whole numbers...

Q2 **31.9 g** of **aluminium** reacts with **288.1 g** of **bromine** to form a compound. Work out the empirical formula of the compound.

(A_r of Al = 27, A_r of Br = 80)

Even though there's no table to help you this time, you still need to use the same steps as you did in the question above.

....

....

....

....

Q3 Work out the empirical formula of the compound made when **72.0 g** of calcium reacts with **127.8 g** of **chlorine**.

(A_r of Ca = 40, A_r of Cl = 35.5)

....

....

....

....

Percentage Yield

Q1 James did an experiment to make **silver chloride** (AgCl). **1.2 g** of silver chloride was produced.

a) Explain what is meant by the **yield** of a chemical reaction.

....

b) The formula for calculating the **percentage yield** of a reaction is:

$$\text{percentage yield} = \frac{\text{actual yield}}{\text{theoretical yield}} \times 100$$

The theoretical yield is the yield that you expect to get.

James calculated that he should get **2.7 g** of silver chloride. What was the **percentage yield**?

....

Q2 Aaliya is taking part in a chemistry competition at school. She has to carry out a chemical reaction to make as much **product** as possible.

Chemistry Competition
LAURA — 56%
ANDREW — 38%
LOUISE — 79%
CUTHBERT — 1%
AALIYA —
Barry
smells

a) Aaliya calculated that she should make **15 g** of product.
But after doing the reaction she only got **6 g**.
Calculate the **percentage yield** for Aaliya's reaction.

....

b) The scoreboard on the right shows the percentage yield for the other students. Who has **won** the competition?

....

Q3 Four samples of magnesium were burned to make magnesium oxide. The **expected** yield was **3.33 g**.

Sample	Mass of oxide (g)
A	3.00
B	3.18
C	3.05
D	3.15

a) The mass of magnesium oxide produced from each sample is shown in the table. What is the percentage yield for each sample?

A. ....

B. ....

C. ....

D. ....

b) Which of the following could be reasons why the yield was not 100%? Circle **two** letters.

A Some of the oxide was lost before it was weighed.   **B** Too much magnesium was burned.

C Not all of the magnesium was burned.   **D** The reaction was too fast.

Percentage Yield

Q4   Complete the table of results showing the **percentage yields** from different experiments.

You can use the space below for working out.

Actual yield	Theoretical yield	Percentage yield
3.4 g	4.0 g	**a)**
6.4 g	7.2 g	**b)**
3.6 g	4.5 g	**c)**
5.9 g	6.5 g	**d)**

Q5   Fill in the gaps to complete the passage below using the words from the box.

waste   expensive   harmful   useful   environment

Chemical reactions can produce lots of unwanted .... products.

These products are not commercially .... so they can not be sold

to make money. They can also be .... and may pose a threat to

the .... It can be .... to dispose

of these products safely.

Q6   Limestone is made up of **calcium carbonate**. When **100 tonnes** of
limestone were heated, **42 tonnes** of solid **calcium oxide** were made.

a)   The theoretical yield of the reaction was **56 tonnes**.
Calculate the percentage yield.

....

....

b)   Limestone is **not** a **pure** substance — it doesn't just contain calcium carbonate.
Explain how this may affect the percentage yield given by the reaction.

....

....

83

Mixed Questions — C2b Topics 4, 5 & 6

Q1 The results of a reaction between **calcium carbonate** and **hydrochloric acid** are shown on the graph.

a) Which part of the curve shows the fastest rate of reaction — A, B or C? ....

b) Explain what happens to the reaction at point C.

....

....

c) At 35 °C, the reaction followed the curve shown on the graph. Draw **two** other complete curves on the same diagram to show how the rate of reaction might change at 25 °C and 45 °C.

d) Give **three** factors other than temperature that affect the rate of reaction.

....

Q2 The elements of **Group 1**, the alkali metals, are **reactive** metals.

The elements are in the same order here as they are in the periodic table.

Group 1 Elements
Lithium
Sodium
Potassium
Rubidium
Caesium
Francium

a) Choose an **element** from the list to answer each of these questions.

i) the least reactive element. ....

ii) the element that has the fastest reaction with water. ....

b) Complete the following sentences by circling the correct word in each pair.

Group 1 metals react with **water / air** to produce **hydrogen / oxygen** gas.

The **hydroxide / chloride** solutions formed by Group 1 metals in water are **acidic / alkaline**.

Q3 **Iodine** vapour reacts with **hydrogen** to form hydrogen iodide.

I I + H H → H I H I

a) Which old bonds are broken? ....

b) Which new bonds are made? ....

c) Which of the processes is endothermic — breaking bonds or forming new ones?

....

d) Overall the reaction is endothermic. Do you think that the temperature of the reaction mixture will rise or fall during this reaction? Explain your answer.

....

....

C2b Topic 6 — Quantitative Chemistry

Mixed Questions — C2b Topics 4, 5 & 6

Q4   Metals make up about 80% of all the elements in the periodic table.

a)   Shade the area where **transition metals** are found on the periodic table.

b)   Read each of the following statements about metals. If the statement is **true**, tick the box.

☐ Metals are generally malleable.

☐ All metals form coloured compounds.

☐ All metals conduct electricity.

☐ Generally, metals have low melting and boiling points.

Q5   Orwell found that **1.4 g** of **silicon** reacted with **7.1 g** of **chlorine** to make silicon chloride.

a)   Work out the **empirical formula** of the silicon chloride. (A_r of Si = 28, A_r of Cl = 35.5)

....

....

....

b)   Calculate the **percentage mass** of chlorine in silicon chloride.

$$\% \text{ mass} = \frac{A_r \times \text{No. of atoms (of that element)}}{M_r \text{ (of whole compound)}} \times 100$$

....

....

c)   Orwell expected the reaction to produce **8.5 g** of silicon chloride, but he only got **6.5 g**. Calculate the percentage yield for this reaction.

$$\% \text{ yield} = \frac{\text{actual yield}}{\text{theoretical yield}} \times 100$$

....

Q6   **Aqueous chlorine**, Cl_2, was added to **potassium bromide solution**, KBr. Aqueous chlorine is pale green and potassium bromide is colourless.

a)   Complete and **balance** the following chemical equation:

Cl_2 + ... KBr $\rightarrow$ .... + ...

b)   What colour change would you see when the two reactants are mixed?

....

c)   Suggest why bromine solution will **not** react with aqueous potassium chloride.

....

Static Electricity

Q1 Label this diagram of an **atom** using the words below.

electron

protons

nucleus

neutrons

....

....

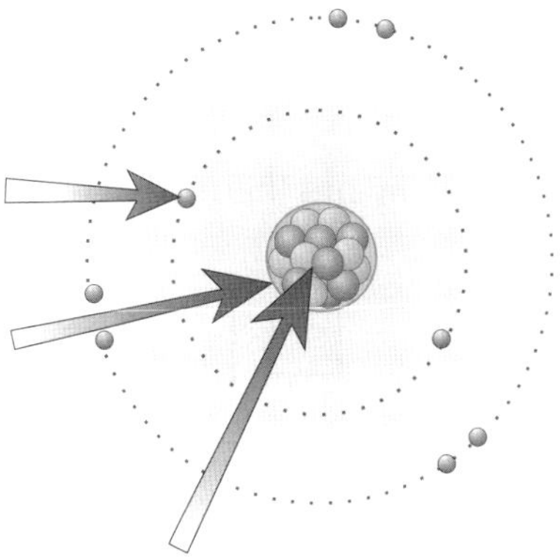

.... and ....

Q2 Circle the pairs of charges that would **attract** each other.

positive and positive   positive and negative   negative and positive   negative and negative

Q3 Complete the passage by using the words in the box below.

static	friction	electrons	positive	insulating	negative

.... electricity can build up when two ....

materials are rubbed together. The .... moves ....

from one material onto the other. This leaves a .... charge

on one of the materials and a .... charge on the other.

Q4 Complete this table to show the relative **charges** and **masses** of each particle.

Particle	Mass	Charge
	1	+1
Neutron	1	
Electron		−1

Static Electricity

Q5 Russell hears a crackling noise when he takes off his new jumper.
The crackling noise is made by charges on his clothes rearranging themselves.

Why are there charges on Russell's clothes? Tick the box next to the correct explanation.

☐ The friction when Russell takes off his jumper transfers electrons from his clothes to his jumper.

☐ The friction when Russell takes off his jumper causes electrons to jump from the air onto Russell.

☐ The friction when Russell takes off his jumper transfers protons from his clothes to his jumper.

Q6 a) Draw lines to match up the start and end of each sentence to describe what happens in a **thunderstorm**.

A — If the voltage gets big enough...

B — The bottoms of the clouds become negatively charged...

C — As the charge increases...

D — Raindrops and ice bump together...

... the voltage gets higher and higher.

... and electrons are transferred between them.

... there is a huge spark (a flash of lightning).

... because they gain extra electrons.

b) Put the sentences (A – D) in the correct order by writing the letters below.

1. ....

2. ....

3. ....

4. ....

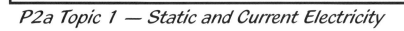

P2a Topic 1 — Static and Current Electricity

Static Electricity

Q7 Tick the boxes to show whether the statements below are **true** or **false**.

	True	False

a) A charged comb can pick up small pieces of paper if they are placed near it.

b) A charged object can force electrons in an uncharged object to move — this is called induction.

c) Electrically charged objects can attract other objects — but only if they are charged too.

Q8 Wayne rubs a balloon against his jumper.

a) Wayne has given the balloon a **negative** charge. Which way must the electrons have moved to give the balloon its charge? Circle the correct word from each pair to complete the answer.

> Electrons must have moved from **the balloon** / **Wayne's jumper**
>
> onto **the balloon** / **Wayne's jumper**.

b) After rubbing the balloon on his jumper, Wayne holds it up against a wall and it sticks. Explain, in terms of charges, why the balloon sticks to the **uncharged** wall.

....

....

....

Q9 Jonny walks across a **nylon** carpet wearing trainers with **insulating soles**. When he goes to open the **metal** door handle he gets an electric shock. Explain why.

....

....

....

....

Top Tips: Static electricity is responsible for many of life's little annoyances — bad hair days, and those little shocks you get from touching car doors and even stroking the cat. Still, it can be kinda cool too — thunderstorms can be spectacular and hours of fun can be had with a balloon...

Uses and Dangers of Static Electricity

Q1   Complete the passage using the words below.

explosion   tankers   spark   earthed

> Static electricity can be dangerous when refuelling aircraft. If too much static
>
> builds up, there might be a(n) .... which could cause a(n)
>
> .... To prevent this happening, the nozzle of the filler pipe
>
> is .... so the charge is conducted away. There are similar
>
> safety problems with fuel .... and at petrol stations.

Q2   The sentences below are wrong. Write out a **correct** version for each sentence.

a)   When fuel tankers are being refuelled they are earthed using an insulator.

....

....

b)   If a positively charged object is earthed, the electrons flow from the object to the ground.

....

....

Q3   A bike frame is painted using an **electrostatic paint sprayer**.

a)   Circle the correct word in each pair to complete the
passage on spray painting using static electricity.

> The spray gun is charged. It charges the small drops of paint with the
>
> **same / opposite** charge. These paint drops are **repelled by / attracted to**
>
> one another, so a very fine spray is produced. The object being painted
>
> has the **same / opposite** charge as the gun, so it **attracts / repels** the paint
>
> — this gives an even coat.

b)   Give **one** other use of electrostatic sprayers.

....

Charge and Current

Q1 There are two types of current: **direct current** (d.c.) and **alternating current** (a.c.).

a) Circle the correct description of **direct current**.

Current that keeps flowing in the same direction.

Current that keeps changing direction.

b) Circle all the power supplies from the list below that supply **direct current**.

cells   batteries   wall sockets

Q2 Complete the passage using words from the box below.

You won't need to use all of the words.

metal	slowly	rate	electrons	protons	quickly

Current is the .... of flow of charge. This is just how

.... the charge flows. In a .... the

current is a flow of ....

Q3 The table below shows the **time** three lamps are left on for and the **current** passing through each one. Fill in the table by calculating the missing values for **charge**.

charge = current × time

	Lamp A	Lamp B	Lamp C
Time (s)	2	4	5
Current (A)	3	3	2
Charge (C)			

Q4 A battery can supply a current of **5 A** for **20 minutes** before it needs recharging. Calculate how much **charge** the battery can provide before it needs recharging.

First you need to change 20 minutes into seconds.

....

....

....

Electric Current and Potential Difference

Q1 Use the words in the box to fill in the gaps. Use each word once only.

| more | potential difference | resistance | less | current | force |

a) The flow of electrons round a circuit is called the ....

b) .... is the .... that pushes the current round the circuit.

c) If you increase the potential difference, ... current will flow.

d) If you increase the ...., ... current will flow.

\\\ \ \ | | / / / /,
Potential difference is
the same as voltage.
/ / / | | \ \ \ \ \

Q2 The following statements are wrong.
Write out a correct version of each.

a) The smaller the potential difference, the bigger the current.

....

b) Resistance is anything in a circuit which speeds up the flow of charge.

....

c) Potential difference is measured in amperes.

....

d) Potential difference is conserved at circuit junctions.

....

Q3 The diagram opposite shows a **parallel** circuit. Ammeter A_2 has a reading of **0.27 A** and A_3 has a reading of **0.43 A**.

What reading is shown on ammeter A_1?
Circle the correct answer.

0.16 A   0.7 A   0.43 A

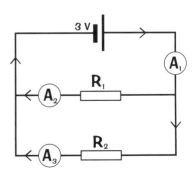

Resistance and V = I × R

Q1 Tick the boxes to show whether these statements are **true** or **false**.

True False

a) The current in a circuit can be changed using a variable resistor. ☐ ☐

b) An ammeter should be connected in parallel with a component. ☐ ☐

c) Items that are in series can be in any order in the circuit. ☐ ☐

d) A voltmeter should be connected in series with a component. ☐ ☐

Q2 **Resistance**, **potential difference** and **current** are all dependent on each other.

Fill in the missing values in the table below.

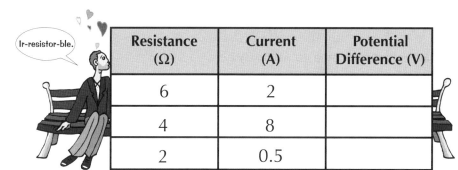

Resistance (Ω)	Current (A)	Potential Difference (V)
6	2	
4	8	
2	0.5	

Q3 Fabio sets up a standard circuit using a **variable resistor** to test the resistance of a component.

a) Label the standard test circuit using the words in the box below.

voltmeter   component
variable resistor   ammeter

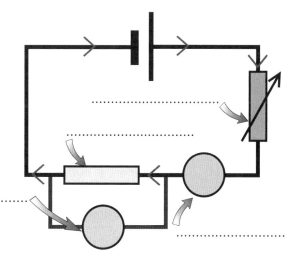

b) The component has a resistance of **2.5 Ω**.
Fabio measures a current of **2.4 A**. Calculate the potential difference across the component.

....

....

**Electrical Devices and Resistance**

Q1   Write the correct label under each of the **V-I graphs** below. Use words from the list.

FIXED RESISTOR   FILAMENT LAMP   DIODE

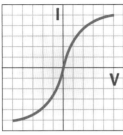   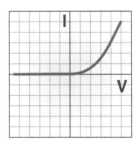   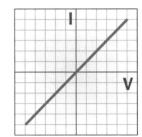

A ....   B ....   C ....

Q2   Tick the boxes to show whether the following are **true** or **false**.

		True	False
a)	The resistance of a filament lamp decreases as it gets hot.	☐	☐
b)	Current can flow freely through a diode in both directions.	☐	☐
c)	The current through a fixed resistor at constant temperature is proportional to the potential difference.	☐	☐
d)	Current can flow both ways through a filament lamp.	☐	☐
e)	An LDR has a high resistance in very bright light.	☐	☐
f)	The resistance of a thermistor increases as the temperature decreases.	☐	☐

Q3   Leyla was doing her homework when the **light** on her desk **went out**. Leyla's mum says the **bulb** has blown and needs replacing, but that they should wait till it **cools down** before touching it.

a)   Why is the bulb hot? Circle the answer.

> A — When a bulb blows it causes a small explosion which heats the bulb.

> B — When there is current through the bulb there is an energy transfer which heats the bulb.

> C — When the current stops flowing through a bulb the energy is transferred to heat.

b)   Give **two** disadvantages of this heating effect.

1. ....

2. ....

Top Tips: Wow... diodes, thermistors, LDRs, current, energy AND filament bulbs — this page really is full to the brim with physics joy. Make sure you know all you need to know about it.

P2a Topic 2 — Controlling and Using Electric Current

Electrical Power and Energy

Q1 Fill in the gaps using the words in the box.

power	current	how long	potential

The total energy transferred by an appliance depends on

.... it's used for and its ....

The power of an appliance can be calculated using the formula:

power = ... difference × ....

Q2 An electric heater is rated at **230 V**, **6.5 A**.
Calculate its power. Circle the correct answer below.

35.4 W   1495 W   35.4 kW   1495 kW

Q3 Dale loves a bit of DIY, and is drilling holes to put up some shelves.
His electric drill is attached to a **12 V** battery and uses a current of **2.3 A**.

If it takes Dale 30 seconds to drill a hole, how much energy
will be transferred by the motor each time he drills a hole?

$E = V \times I \times t$

....

....

Q4 Lucy is comparing **three lamps**. She connects each lamp in a circuit
and measures the **current**. Her results are shown in the table below.

Complete the table by filling in the missing values.

	Lamp A	Lamp B	Lamp C
Potential Difference (V)	12	3	230
Current (A)	2.5	4	0.1
Power (W)			
Energy transferred in one minute (J)			

Don't forget to change
the time to seconds.

Velocity and Acceleration

Q1   Which of the following are **vector quantities**? Circle the correct answers.

displacement   speed   velocity

distance   acceleration

Q2   I rode my bike **1500 m** to the shops. It took me **5 minutes**.

a)   Calculate how many seconds there are in 5 minutes.

....

b)   What was my average speed in m/s?

....

....

Q3   Ealing is about **12 km** west of Marble Arch. It takes a
tube train **1200 s** to get to Marble Arch from Ealing.

Only **one** of the following statements is true. Circle the appropriate letter.

A   The average speed of the train is 60 m/s.

B   The average velocity of the train is 10 m/s.

C   The average velocity of the train is 60 m/s due east.

D   The average speed of the train is 10 m/s.

E   The average velocity of the train is 10 m/s due west.

Q4   An egg is dropped from the top of the Eiffel tower.
It hits the ground after **8 seconds**, at a speed of **80 m/s**.

$a = (v - u) \div t$

Calculate the egg's acceleration. Assume it starts from rest.

....

....

Q5   A car accelerates from a speed of **16 m/s** to a speed of **24 m/s** in **4 seconds**.

Calculate the acceleration of the car.

....

....

D-T and V-T Graphs

Q1 Fill in the gaps in these sentences with the words below.
You may use each word once, more than once or not at all.

distance travelled	speed	acceleration

The gradient of a distance-time graph gives you the ....

The gradient of a velocity-time graph gives you the ....

A flat section on a velocity-time graph represents a constant ....

Q2 Write each **letter** from the distance-time graph next to the correct description of motion.

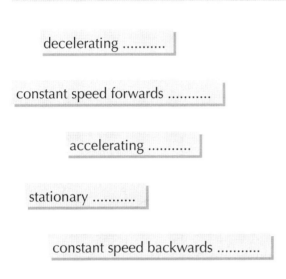

decelerating ....

constant speed forwards ....

accelerating ....

stationary ....

constant speed backwards ....

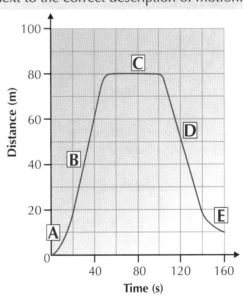

Q3 Steve walked to football training only to find that he'd left his boots at home.
He turned round and walked back home, where he spent 30 seconds looking for
them. To make it to training on time he had to run back at twice his walking speed.

Below is an incomplete **distance-time graph** for Steve's journey.

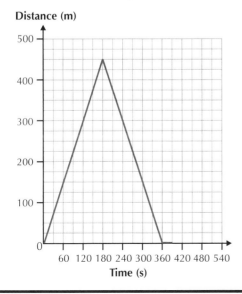

a) How long did it take Steve to walk to training?

....

b) Calculate Steve's speed (in m/s) as he
walked to training.

....

....

c) Complete the graph to show Steve's run back
from his house to training (with his boots).

P2a Topic 3 — Motion and Forces

<u>D-T and V-T Graphs</u>

Q4 Describe the **type of motion** happening at each of the labelled points on the velocity-time graph.

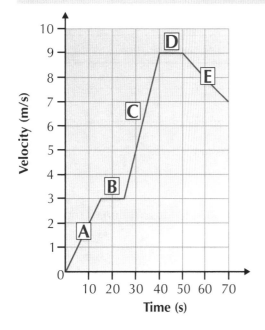

(A) ....

(B) ....

(C) ....

(D) ....

(E) ....

Q5 The velocity-time graph on the right shows the journeys of three different cyclists, A, B and C.

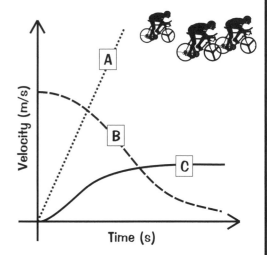

a) Which cyclist is decelerating? ....

b) Which cyclist reaches a constant velocity? ....

c) Which cyclist has the largest acceleration? ....

d) Which cyclist has the lowest final velocity? ....

e) Which cyclist has a constant acceleration? ....

Q6 Below is a velocity-time graph for a spacecraft.

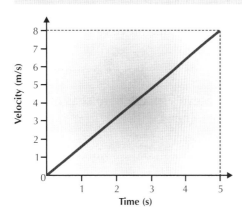

Use the graph to calculate the spacecraft's acceleration.

....

....

....

Top Tips: Don't let all these distance-time and velocity-time graphs get the better of you — break them down into separate chunks and they'll be a whole lot easier to work out. I promise.

Forces

Q1 The forces acting on a balloon floating at a constant height are shown by the **force diagram** below.

The sentences below describe the balloon's motion.
Circle the correct word(s) in each sentence.

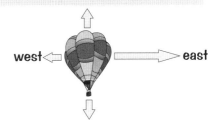

a) There is a greater driving force in the **east / west** direction.

b) The balloon will **rise / fall / stay at the same height**.

Q2 A bear rides a bike north at a constant speed.

a) Label the forces acting on the bear.
Use words from the box below.

> Weight   Reaction
> Drag   Driving Force

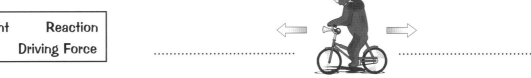

....

....

....

b) The bear brakes and slows down.
Circle the direction of the
overall force in the list below.

forwards / backwards / upwards / downwards

....

Q3 Jane picks up a teapot and hangs it from the ceiling.

a) Label the forces acting on the teapot suspended by the rope on the picture below.

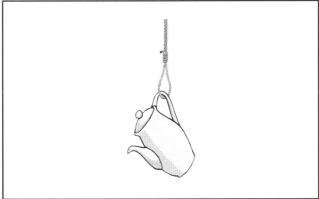

Show the direction of each force and make sure the size of each arrow relates to the size of the force.

b) The rope breaks and the teapot accelerates towards the floor.

i) Are the vertical forces balanced? Explain your answer.

....

ii) The teapot hits the floor without breaking and bounces upwards.
Which force causes the teapot to bounce upwards?

....

Think about which force acts upwards on the teapot when it reaches the floor.

<u>*Weight and Terminal Velocity*</u>

Q1   Use the words supplied to fill in the blanks in the paragraph.

terminal	balances	increases	constant
greater		accelerates	

An object is dropped from a height and falls through the atmosphere.

At first, its weight is .... than the air resistance acting on it, so it

.... downwards. As its speed increases, the air resistance

.... until it .... its weight. At this point, its

velocity is .... — its acceleration is zero and the object is said

to have reached its .... velocity.

Q2   A scientist plans to travel to the moon to perform an experiment. He will drop a **hammer** and a **feather** from the same height.

The moon's atmosphere is so thin you can treat it as a vacuum.

Which object will land first? Circle the answer.

feather   hammer   They will both land at the same time.

Q3   A **5 kg** bowling ball is hung on a spring balance and taken to several different planets.

a) What is the weight of the ball on Earth? (Take g = 10 N/kg.)

$W = m \times g$

....

b) Complete the table below to show the weight of the bowling ball on the surfaces of Mercury, Venus, Pluto and Europa.

Location	Gravitational Field Strength (N/kg)	Weight of Bowling Ball (N)
Mercury	3.7	
Venus	8.9	
Pluto	0.6	
Europa (a moon of Jupiter)	1.3	

Forces and Motion

Q1 Tick the correct boxes to show whether the sentences are **true** or **false**.

True False

a) A resultant force is the overall force acting on a body. ☐ ☐

b) An object will remain stationary if there is zero resultant force acting on it. ☐ ☐

c) For an object to keep travelling at a steady speed, it must have an overall force acting on it. ☐ ☐

d) If all the forces on an object are balanced, it is said to have a resultant force acting on it. ☐ ☐

Q2 A **flamingo** is standing on one leg.

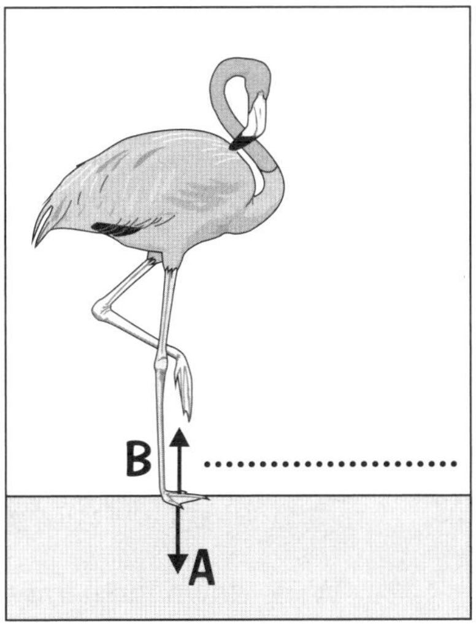

a) Two forces, A and B, are shown on the diagram to the right. Label the force marked B.

b) Complete the following sentences about the two forces:

> Force A is exerted by the .... on the
>
> .... Force B is exerted by the
>
> .... on the ....

c) Are force A and force B equal in size? Explain your answer.

....

....

Q3 Otto is driving the school bus at a **steady speed** along a level road.
Tick the boxes next to any of the following statements which are **true**.

☐ The driving force of the engine is bigger than the friction and air resistance combined.

☐ The driving force of the engine is equal to the friction and air resistance combined.

☐ There are no forces acting on the bus.

☐ No force is required to keep the bus moving.

Force and Acceleration

Q1 Use the words below to fill in the blanks.

mass	force	accelerates	resultant

If an object has a .... force acting on it, it ....

in the direction of the .... The acceleration depends on the size

of the force and on the .... of the object.

Q2 State whether the **forces** acting on these objects are **balanced** (zero resultant force) or **unbalanced**. Explain your answers.

a) A **cricket ball** slowing down as it rolls along the outfield.

....

b) A **vase** knocked off a window ledge.

....

c) A **bag of rubbish** which was dumped into empty space.

There's no air resistance or gravity in empty space.

....

....

Q3 The table below shows the **masses** and **maximum accelerations** of four different antique cars.

Write down the names of the four cars in order of increasing driving force. (Use the lines below the table for your working out.)

1. ....

2. ....

3. ....

4. ....

F = m × a

Car	Mass (kg)	Maximum acceleration (m/s²)
Disraeli 9000	800	5
Palmerston 6i	1560	0.7
Heath TT	950	3
Asquith 380	790	2

....

....

....

....

Force and Acceleration

Q4   A camper van drives along a straight, level road at a **constant speed**.
At this speed, air resistance is **2000 N** and the friction between the wheel bearings is **500 N**.

   a)   What force is the engine exerting?

....

   b)   Draw a diagram to show
all the horizontal forces
acting on the camper van.
Give the size of each force.

Q5   Jen and Sarah want to investigate the relationship between **force** and **acceleration**.
They set up the experiment shown below.

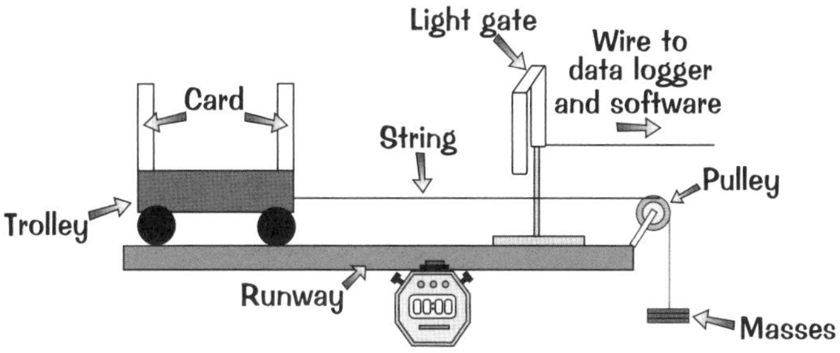

   a)   Number the steps of their experiment 1-4 to put them in order:

☐   The data logging software works out the initial and final velocity of the trolley.

☐   The light gate detects each piece of card as it passes through.

☐   The masses pull the trolley with a constant force so it accelerates.

☐   The acceleration is calculated using the initial and final velocities and the time
taken for the trolley to pass though the light gate.

   b)   Describe the **relationship** between force and acceleration you would expect them to find.

....

Q6   Maisie pulls a **1.5 kg** mass along a table so that it accelerates at **0.25 m/s^2**.

   a)   Calculate the resultant force acting on the mass.
$F = m \times a$

....

....

   b)   Maisie pulls with a force of **0.4 N**. Calculate the force of **friction** between the mass and the table.

....

Mixed Questions — P2a Topics 1, 2 & 3

Q1   Norman loves trainspotting. As a special treat, he not only notes
the train numbers but plots a **distance-time** graph for two of the trains.

a)   For how long is train 2 stationary?

....

b)   Both trains start at a steady speed.
How can you tell this from the graph?

....

c)   Calculate the initial speed of the faster train.

....

d)   Describe the motion of train 1 between 40 s and 80 s.

....

Q2   In the film 'Crouching Sparrow, Hidden Beaver',
a dummy is dropped from the top of a building.

a)   Sketch a **velocity-time graph** for the dummy from the
moment it is dropped until just after it hits the ground.
(Ignore air resistance and assume the dummy does not reach a terminal velocity.)

b)   Do any forces act on the dummy when it lies still on the ground (after falling)? If so, what are they?

....

c)   The take doesn't go to plan so the dummy is lifted back to the top of the building using a motor.
If the motor uses the mains voltage (**230 V**) and a current of **3.3 A**, calculate its power. $P = I \times V$

....

....

d)   The film's director decides to use a taller building for the scene. Falling from this new building,
the dummy reaches its terminal velocity. Explain what is meant by 'terminal velocity'.

....

....

....

Mixed Questions — P2a Topics 1, 2 & 3

Q3 Scott water-skis over a 100 m course. When he reaches the end of the course, Scott lets go of the tow rope.

a) The graph below shows how Scott's speed changed over the course. Describe his **acceleration**:

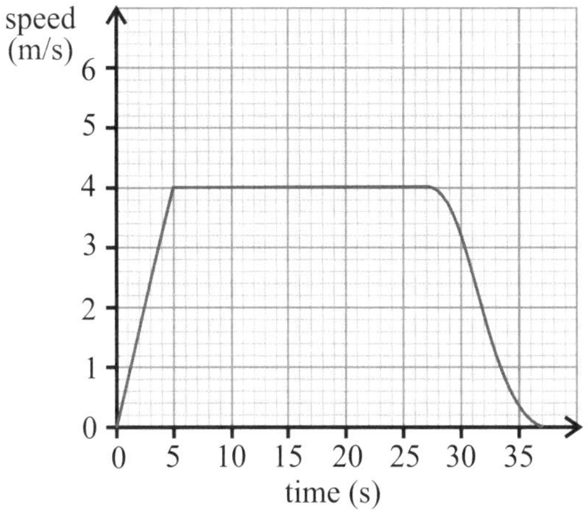

   i) between 0 and 5 seconds,

   ....

   ii) between 5 and 25 seconds,

   ....

   iii) after 30 seconds.

   ....

speed (m/s) vs time (s)

b) Scott is being pulled with a force of **475 N**.

   i) What was the **total combined force** of air resistance and friction between his water skis and the water between 10 and 25 seconds?

   ....

   ii) Explain your answer.

   ....

   ....

Q4 Paul sets off from a junction on his scooter at an acceleration of **1.5 m/s²**. The total mass of Paul and his scooter is **180 kg**. For the following questions, ignore air resistance.

a) What is the driving force of Paul's scooter. Circle the correct answer.

   $F = m \times a$

   120 N   **181.5 N**   **270 N**

b) Calculate the size of the force produced when Paul applies his brakes and decelerates at **5 m/s²**.

   ....

   ....

c) Paul reaches a speed of **17.5 m/s** then accelerates again to a speed of **20 m/s** in **10 seconds**. Calculate his acceleration.

   $a = (v - u) \div t$

   ....

   ....

Mixed Questions — P2a Topics 1, 2 & 3

Q5   The diagram shows an aircraft being refuelled.
No safety precautions have been taken.

a)   **i)**   Explain how static electricity could cause an explosion in this situation.

....

....

ii)   Give one precaution that can be taken to avoid this danger.

....

b)   Write down one example of how static electricity is **useful**.

....

Q6   A temperature sensor containing a thermistor is used to monitor the temperature
of a room. The sensor is connected to a circuit containing a filament bulb.
As the temperature increases, the bulb's brightness increases.

a)   What is a thermistor?

....

b)   Explain why the filament in the bulb glows when a current flows through it.

....

....

....

c)   The filament bulb is connected to a **25 V** electricity supply. A current of **4 A** flows through it.

i)   Calculate how much energy is transferred by the bulb over a time period of **5 minutes**.

$E = I \times V \times t$

....

....

ii)   Calculate how much charge passes through the bulb in this time. $Q = I \times t$

....

....

d)   The sensor uses a **d.c.** electricity supply. Explain, in terms of the flow of charge, what this means.

....

....

Stopping Distances

Q1   **Stopping distance** and **braking distance** are not the same thing.
Complete the definitions below by circling the correct words.

a) Braking distance is the distance the car travels under
the **braking force / driving force** before it comes to a stop.

b) Thinking distance is the distance the car travels during the driver's **braking time / reaction time**.

c) Stopping distance is the **difference between / sum of** the thinking distance and braking distance.

Q2   Will the following factors affect **thinking** distance, **braking** distance or **both**?
Write them in the correct columns in the table below.

tiredness   road surface   weather   speed   mass of the vehicle
alcohol   tyres   brakes   ice

Thinking Distance	Braking Distance

Some factors can be used in both columns.

Q3   Beth finds the **force** needed to slide a 1 kg rubber block across a flat surface
covered in three different materials. The table below shows her results.

a) What force acts to stop the block sliding?

....

Material	Force needed for block to slide
1	60 N
2	5 N
3	24 N

b) Which material (1–3) would provide the most grip for a toy car?

....

c) Beth puts washing-up liquid on Material 3 and repeats the experiment.

i)   What do you expect will happen to the size of the force needed to slide the block?
Circle the correct answer.

increase   decrease   stay the same

ii) Explain your answer.

....

Car Safety

Q1   Circle the correct words or phrases to make the following statements **true**.

a)   If the velocity of a moving object increases, its **mass** / **momentum** will increase.

b)   If you drop a suitcase out of a moving car, the car's momentum will **decrease** / **increase**.

c)   When two objects collide the total momentum **changes** / **stays the same**.

d)   Momentum is a **vector** / **scalar** quantity.

Q2   Complete the passage below using the words from the box.

longer	increasing	small	momentum

When a force acts on an object, it causes a change in ....

When an object changes momentum over a .... amount of time,

it experiences a large force. The .... it takes for the momentum to

change, the smaller the force. Bubble wrap acts to reduce the force on fragile objects.

It works by .... the time over which momentum changes happen.

Q3   Calculate the momentum of the truck below.

velocity = 20 m/s west
mass = 4000 kg

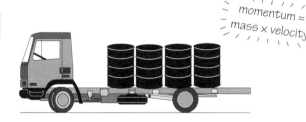

momentum =
mass × velocity

....

....

Q4   For each of the **car safety features** below, draw a line to match it to
the description of the way it helps to protect passengers in a crash.

Crumple zones

Seat belts

Airbags

These stretch slightly, increasing the time for the
passengers to stop and reducing the force acting on them.

These slow down the passengers over a longer
time to reduce the forces on them and stop
them from hitting hard surfaces in the car.

These squash up on impact, increasing the time taken
for the car to stop and reducing the force of the crash.

Car Safety

Q5 Shopping trolley A has a mass of **10 kg** and is moving **east** at **4 m/s**. It collides with trolley B which has a mass of **30 kg** and is moving **west** at **1 m/s**. The two trolleys join together.

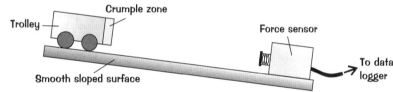

a) Complete the diagram on the right showing the masses and velocities of the trolleys **before** they collide.

b) Calculate the **total momentum** of the trolleys **before** the collision.

....

....

c) What is the momentum of the trolleys **after** the collision as they move away together? Explain your answer.

....

....

Q6 Simon is investigating **crumple zones** using the apparatus shown on the right.

Simon fits the front of a trolley with different materials to make different 'crumple zones'. For each test, the trolley starts **at rest** at the **same position** on the slope and rolls towards the force sensor. The **mass** of the trolley is the **same** in each test. Simon records the **maximum force** of the trolley on the sensor, and **how long** each collision lasts for in the table below.

Crumple zone material	Maximum force during the collision (N)	Collision time (s)
1	10	0.8
2	40	0.2
3	16	0.5

a) Describe the **relationship** between the **collision time** and the **maximum force** during the collision.

....

....

b) Which of the crumple zone materials (1–3) worked best? Explain your answer.

....

....

....

Work and Power

Q1   Circle the correct words in the following sentences.

a)   Work involves the transfer of **force** / **energy**.

b)   To do work **a force** / **an acceleration** must act over a **distance** / **time**.

c)   Work is measured in **watts** / **joules**.

Q2   Tick the boxes to show whether the following statements are **true** or **false**.

		True	False
a)	Work is done when a toy car is pushed along the ground.	☐	☐
b)	No work is done if a force is applied to an object which does not move.	☐	☐
c)	Gravity does work on an apple that is not moving.	☐	☐
d)	Gravity does work on an apple that falls out of a tree.	☐	☐

Q3   Complete this passage by using the words provided.
The words can be used more than once.

energy	joules	power	light	watts

………….......…………. is the rate of doing work, or how much ………….......…………

is transferred per second. It is measured in ………….......………… (or ………….......…………

per second). A 100 W light bulb transfers 100 ………….......………… of electrical energy

into ………….......………… and heat each second.

Q4   An elephant exerts a constant force of **1200 N** to push a donkey along a track. $E = F \times d$

a)   Calculate the work done by the elephant if the donkey moves **8 m**.

....

....

b)   From where does the elephant get the energy to do this work?

....

Top Tips: Power is a measure of the energy transferred, or work done, within a certain time — the faster a person or machine can get a task done, the more powerful it is. Just think, if you were a power-mad ruler you could try take over the world in the blink of an eye, mwah haa ha ha ha...

Work and Power

Q5 Catherine and Sally run up a set of stairs to see who can get to the top more quickly. At the top of the stairs, Catherine has done **2300 J** of work, and Sally has done **2400 J** of work.

$P = E \div t$

Catherine won the race in **6.2 s**, while Sally took **6.4 s**. Which girl generated more **power**?

....

....

Q6 Tom likes to build model boats. His favourite boat is the Carter, which has a motor power of **150 W**.

$E = P \times t$

a) Calculate how much **energy** the Carter transfers in **600 seconds**.

....

....

b) Tom decides to get a model speed boat which transfers **120 000 J** in **600 seconds**. Calculate the **power** of the engine.

....

....

Q7 Ben climbs up a ladder.

a) What force(s) is Ben doing work **against** as he climbs? Circle the correct answer.

gravity   driving force   power

b) How much work does Ben do when he climbs **5 m** against a force of **600 N**?

....

....

....

c) Calculate Ben's power output if he climbs the ladder in **15 seconds**.

....

....

Kinetic and Potential Energy

Q1   Tick the boxes to show whether the following statements are **true** or **false**.

		True	False
a)	Gravitational potential energy = mass × g × height.	☺	☹
b)	Kinetic energy is energy due to an object's position.	☺	☹
c)	On Earth, the gravitational field strength is approximately 20 N/kg.	☺	☹
d)	The kinetic energy of an object depends on its velocity.	☺	☹

Q2   Number the following vehicles 1-3, where 1 is the vehicle carrying the **most kinetic energy**, and 3 is the vehicle carrying the **least kinetic energy**.

$$K.E = \tfrac{1}{2} \times m \times v^2$$

60 000 kg, 17 m/s	100 kg, 8 m/s	1200 kg, 15 m/s

....

Working-out space →

....

....

....

Q3   Dave lifts **28** flagstones onto the delivery truck. Each flagstone has a mass of **25 kg** and has to be lifted **1.2 m** onto the truck.

a)   How much **gravitational potential energy** does one flagstone gain when lifted onto the truck? (g = 10 N/kg)

....

....

b)   What is the **total gravitational potential energy** gained by the flagstones after they are all loaded onto the truck?

....

....

Top Tips: My physics teacher once said I had lots of potential... thanks to being sat on a very tall stool. Ah, physics jokes... you've got to love 'em. Kinetic energy and gravitational potential energy crop up everywhere, so make sure you get friendly with their equations.

Conservation of Energy

Q1 A toy cricket ball hit straight upwards has a gravitational potential energy of **242 J** at the **top** of its flight. What is the ball's **kinetic energy** just before it hits the ground? Circle the correct answer.

| 0 J | 121 J | 242 J | 484 J |

Q2 Complete the passage below using the words from the box.

disappears	heat	used	converted	created

The principle of the conservation of energy states that energy can never be ....

nor destroyed — only .... from one form to another. This means that

energy never .... , it just gets transferred to other forms. Most energy

transfers involve some losses, often as .... and sometimes as sound.

This energy is still there, it just can't be .... again easily.

Q3 Dave the frog **jumps** off the ground at a speed of **10 m/s**.

$K.E. = \frac{1}{2} \times m \times v^2$

a) If Dave has a mass of **0.5 kg**, what is his **kinetic energy** as he leaves the ground?

....

b) What is Dave's maximum possible **gravitational potential energy**?

....

....

c) Dave uses the equation for gravitational potential energy to work out the **maximum height** he can jump. Why won't Dave reach this height in practice? Explain your answer in terms of energy.

....

....

Q4 Kim dives off a **5 m** high diving board and belly-flops into the swimming pool below. If Kim's mass is **100 kg**, calculate her kinetic energy as she hits the water (g = 10 N/kg).

$G.P.E. = m \times g \times h$

....

....

Radioactivity

Q1   Complete the passage below using the words in the box.

unstable	radiation	protons	neutrons	decay

Isotopes are atoms with the same number of .... but different

numbers of ....   Some isotopes are ....

These isotopes .... (break down) into other elements and give

out ....

Q2   Tick the boxes to show whether the sentences are **true** or **false**.

                                                                         True   **False**

a)   The number of protons in an atom is known as its atomic number.   ☐   ☐

b)   The number of neutrons in an atom is known as its mass number.   ☐   ☐

c)   Atoms of the same element with the same
number of neutrons are called isotopes.   ☐   ☐

d)   You can predict when radioactive decay will happen.   ☐   ☐

Q3   For each of the isotopes below, give the **number of protons** and the **number of neutrons**.

a) $^{3}_{1}H$

    Protons: ....

    Neutrons: ....

b) $^{14}_{6}C$

    Protons: ....

    Neutrons: ....

c) $^{14}_{7}N$

    Protons: ....

    Neutrons: ....

d) $^{16}_{8}O$

    Protons: ....

    Neutrons: ....

Q4   Each of the sentences below are **wrong**. Write out the correct version of each sentence.

a)   Gamma radiation can pass through thick lead.

    ....

b)   Beta particles are neutrons that come from the nucleus.

    ....

c)   Alpha particles are small, heavy and slow-moving compared to beta and gamma.

    ....

Radioactivity

Q5 Circle the correct words to complete the table below.
Two have been done for you.

Radiation	What is it?	Ionising power	Penetrating power
alpha	electrons / (helium nuclei) / electromagnetic radiation	weak / moderate / strong	(low) / moderate / high
beta	electrons / helium nuclei / electromagnetic radiation	weak / moderate / strong	low / moderate / high
gamma	electrons / helium nuclei / electromagnetic radiation	weak / moderate / strong	low / moderate / high

Q6 Radiation from three sources — A, B and C, was directed towards target sheets
of **paper**, **aluminium** and **lead**. The results of the experiment are shown below.

Source A — some of the radiation was stopped by the lead.
Source B — the radiation was stopped by the paper.
Source C — the radiation was stopped by the aluminium.

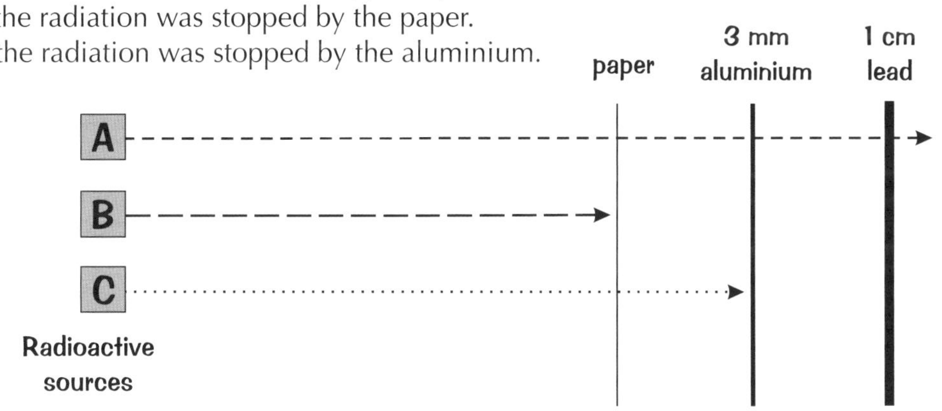

What type of radiation is:

source A? ...., source B? ...., source C? ....

Q7 Atoms can be **ionised** using ionising radiation.

a) Explain what **ionisation** is.

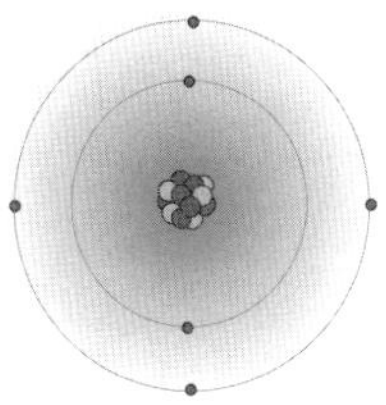

....

....

b) Explain how an **alpha particle** passing by an atom could ionise it.

....

....

Nuclear Fission and Fusion

Q1 Tick the boxes to show whether the statements below are **true** or **false**.

		True	False
a)	Nuclear fusion involves small nuclei joining together.	☐	☐
b)	A nuclear fission reaction releases more energy than a nuclear fusion reaction.	☐	☐
c)	Fusion reactors produce very little radioactive waste.	☐	☐
d)	We use nuclear fusion to generate electricity in the UK.	☐	☐
e)	Stars use nuclear fusion as an energy source.	☐	☐

Q2 a) Circle the correct word in each pair to complete the passage on nuclear fission.

In nuclear fission, a slow-moving **electron / neutron** is fired at an atom of uranium-235 and is absorbed by the nucleus. This makes the atom **stable / unstable** and causes it to split. When the atom splits it forms two new lighter **daughter / son** nuclei and releases energy. The new, lighter nuclei are **explosive / radioactive**.
This process is called a **link / chain** reaction.

b) When atoms split in a nuclear fission reaction, particles are given out that allow the reaction to continue. Circle the name of these particles from the list below.

ions   electrons   alpha particles   neutrons

Q3 In 1989 two scientists claimed to have created energy through **cold fusion**.

Tick **two** boxes next to the reasons why cold fusion has **not** been accepted by the scientific community.

☐ The scientists' work was done too early for people to understand.

☐ The experiment was done in a vacuum which is too difficult to recreate.

☐ The reactions created too much energy for scientists to safely control.

☐ Other scientists tried to repeat the work, but only a few managed to get the same results reliably.

☐ The scientists' work had not been peer reviewed before it was reported.

☐ Other scientists thought the work was pointless and ignored its importance.

P2b Topic 5 — Nuclear Fission and Nuclear Fusion

Nuclear Power Stations

Q1   Label the diagram below with the types of **energy** created at each stage. Use the words in the list.

Kinetic energy   Electrical energy   Nuclear energy   Heat energy

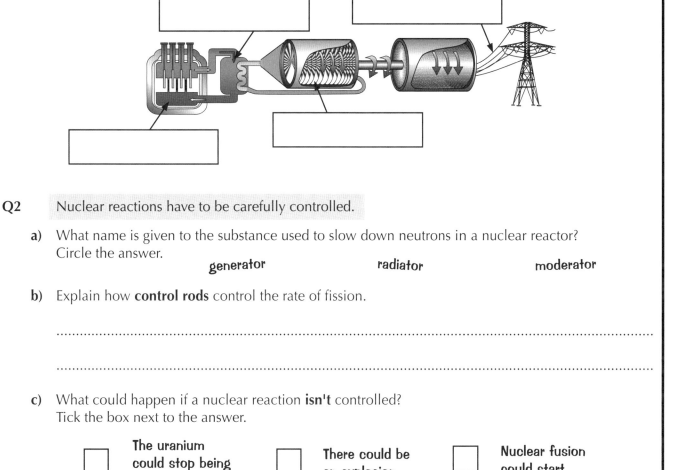

Q2   Nuclear reactions have to be carefully controlled.

a) What name is given to the substance used to slow down neutrons in a nuclear reactor? Circle the answer.

generator   radiator   moderator

b) Explain how **control rods** control the rate of fission.

....

....

c) What could happen if a nuclear reaction **isn't** controlled? Tick the box next to the answer.

☐ The uranium could stop being radioactive.

☐ There could be an explosion.

☐ Nuclear fusion could start.

Q3   Nuclear reactors use heat energy to create **electricity**.

a) What causes the reactor to get hot?

....

b) Describe how heat energy from the reactor is used to generate electricity.

....

....

Top Tips: WOW. Nuclear power is sooo cool. Well, actually it's pretty hot in the reactor but that's by the by. Nuclear power produces loads of energy, doesn't release carbon dioxide and isn't going to run out anytime soon... It would be the perfect energy source if you didn't have to tackle all that dangerous radioactive waste or the possibility of nuclear explosions...

Background Radiation and Half-life

Q1   Complete the passage below using the words in the box.

becquerels	half-life	decreases	zero
second	undecayed	increases	

The activity of a radioactive source .... over time as the

radioactive nuclei decay. However, the activity never reaches .... ,

so scientists use the idea of .... to measure how quickly the activity

falls. This is the time it takes for half the .... nuclei in a radioactive

substance to decay. Activity is measured in .... — 1 Bq is one decay

per ....

You won't need to use all the words.

Q2   Circle the letters of the **true** statements.

   A   Differences in the UK's background radiation are mainly caused by radon gas.

   B   Human activity doesn't contribute to background radiation.

   C   If there were no radioactive substances on Earth, there would be no background radiation.

   D   Cosmic rays from the Sun are a form of background radiation.

Q3   The amount of **radon** gas found in people's homes varies across the UK.
         Why does the concentration vary across the country? Circle the answer.

         It depends on how cold your home is.

         It depends on how far North you live.

         It depends on the type of rock the house is built on.

Q4   A radioactive isotope has a half-life of **60 years**.
         Tick the box next to the correct statement.

         In 60 years, half of the atoms in the material will have gone.   ☐

         In 30 years' time, only half the atoms will be radioactive.   ☐

         In 60 years' time, the activity will be half what it is now.   ☐

         In about 180 years there will be no radioactivity left in the material.   ☐

Calculating Half-life

Q1 Dice can be used to simulate **radioactive decay**. 24 dice are rolled, and any which roll a six are removed — they have "**decayed**". The rest are rolled again, and so on, until all the dice have decayed.

Tick the box next to **one way** in which this experiment is like radioactive decay.

☐ The dice that roll six are like atoms that haven't decayed.

☐ It's random which dice will roll a six, and it's random which atoms will decay.

☐ The dice that are rolled each time are like decayed atoms.

☐ The same number of sixes will be rolled each time, and the same number of atoms decay each second.

Q2 The graph shows how the activity of a radioactive isotope sample decreases with time.

Activity (Bq)

a) The initial activity of the sample was 1200 Bq. What was the activity after 1 half-life.

....

....

b) Use the graph to find the half-life of this isotope.

....

....

c) What was the activity of the sample after **3 half-lives**?

....

....

Q3 A radioactive isotope has a half-life of **40 seconds**.

You'll need to change 4 minutes into seconds.

a) How many half-lives are there in **4 minutes**?

....

....

b) If the initial activity of a sample of the isotope was **8000 Bq**, what would the activity be after **4 minutes**?

....

....

....

....

Uses of Radioactivity

Q1   Circle the correct word(s) in each pair to complete the passage.

> High doses of **radio / gamma** radiation will kill all living cells. Because of this,
> **radio / gamma** radiation is used to treat cancers. Hospital workers have to be
> very careful when treating a patient to direct the radiation **right at / away from**
> the cancerous cells. They do this to try and **reduce / increase** the damage done to
> healthy cells.

Q2   The table shows some information on **radioactive isotopes**.

Which of the isotopes in the table would be most suitable:

a) for a smoke detector?

....

b) to sterilise food?

....

c) to control the thickness of paper?

....

Radioactive isotope	Decays by ...
strontium-90	beta emission
americium-241	mainly alpha emission
cobalt-60	beta and gamma emission

Q3   Number the sentences in order (1– 5) to explain how a **smoke detector** works.
The first one has been done for you.

☐	The current stops flowing.
1	The radioactive source emits alpha radiation.
☐	The alarm sounds.
☐	A fire starts and smoke absorbs the alpha radiation.
☐	The alpha radiation causes ionisation of the air and a current flows.

?

Top Tips: When you're answering questions about the uses of radioactivity, it's important
that you remember which type is used for which thing. Each of the three types can be dangerous
if used incorrectly, but pretty darned useful in the right place.

Uses of Radioactivity

Q4 Certain radioactive isotopes can be used as **tracers** in the body.

You won't need to use all of the words.

a) Complete the passage using the words below.

cancer   diagnose   swallowed   alpha   detector   beta

A medical tracer is injected into, or .... by, a patient and travels around the body. The tracer's path is followed using a .... outside the body. The reading from the detector is used to spot and .... medical conditions (such as ....). All isotopes which are taken into the body must be .... or gamma emitters so that the radiation passes out of the body.

b) State **one other** use of gamma emitting tracers.

....

Q5 Radiation can be used to **sterilise** surgical instruments.

a) What type of radiation is used to sterilise surgical instruments? Circle the answer.

alpha radiation   beta radiation   gamma radiation

radioactive source

thick lead

b) Similar machines can be used to treat **fruit**.
Explain how irradiating the fruit will help to stop it going bad.

....

....

Q6 The diagram shows how **beta radiation** can be used to control the thickness of paper in a paper mill.

Explain why beta radiation is used rather than alpha or gamma.

radiation source
beta
PAPER
hydraulic control   processor unit   detector

....

....

....

Dangers of Radioactivity

Q1 The three different types of ionising radiation can all be dangerous.

a) Which **two** types of ionising radiation can pass through human skin?
Circle the correct answers.

alpha   beta   gamma

b) Which type of radiation is usually the most dangerous inside the body?

....

c) Tick the boxes to show whether the statements are **true** or **false**.

	True	False
i) Only alpha radiation will enter living cells and collide with molecules.	☐	☐
ii) Interactions between ionising radiation and molecules cause ionisation.	☐	☐
iii) Lower doses of radiation can create mutant cells which multiply.	☐	☐
iv) Low doses of radiation will cause radiation sickness.	☐	☐

Q2 Give **four** ways you can protect yourself when working with **radioactive sources** in the laboratory.

1. ....

2. ....

3. ....

4. ....

Q3 When the radioactive substance **radium** was first discovered, it was used to make luminous paint, which was used in the manufacture of glow-in-the-dark watches.

a) Explain why this was **dangerous** to the watch painters.

....

....

....

b) The use of radium in a range of products went on for over **20 years**.
Explain why it took so long for people to realise it was dangerous.

....

....

....

Nuclear Power

Q1   **Radioactive waste** left over from **nuclear fission** is very difficult to dispose of.

a)   Why is the waste produced by nuclear power stations
a **long-term problem**? Tick the box next to the answer.

Radioactive waste has to be moved every 10 years. ☐

Radioactive waste can have a very long half-life. ☐

Radioactive waste needs to be handled safely which is expensive. ☐

Radioactive waste only emits radiation 10 years after being disposed of. ☐

b)   **Vitrification** is one way of disposing of radioactive waste.
Describe the process of vitrification.

....

....

c)   Why is nuclear waste usually buried deep underground? Circle the answer.

| The waste gives off harmful and smelly gases. | There needs to be lots of stuff to absorb the radiation before it can reach the surface. | The waste needs to be buried where it is cooler so that it doesn't explode. |

Q2   The majority of the UK's electricity is still produced by burning **fossil fuels**.

a)   Is generating electricity using nuclear power **cheaper** than using fossil fuels?
Explain your answer.

....

....

....

b)   Other than costs, write down **two advantages** and **disadvantages** of using nuclear power
instead of using fossil fuels to generate electricity.

Advantages: 1. ....

2. ....

Disadvantages: 1. ....

2. ....

Top Tips: Nuclear power is a tricky subject — there are arguments for and against it.
Make sure you know **both** sides of the argument. That way you can argue with yourself.

P2b Topic 6 — Using Radioactive Materials

<u>*Mixed Questions — P2b Topics 4, 5 & 6*</u>

Q1 Cherie and Tony rob a bank. They escape in a getaway car with a mass of **2100 kg** and travel at a constant speed of **25 m/s** along a straight, level road.

a) Calculate the momentum of the car.

....

....

b) A police car swings into the middle of the road and stops ahead of Cherie's car. Cherie slams on the brakes and comes to a halt.

i) Write down one factor that could affect Cherie's **thinking distance**.

....

ii) Write down one factor that could affect Cherie's **braking distance**.

....

c) How would **seat belts** have helped keep Cherie and Tony safer if they had crashed? Tick the box next to the answer.

Seat belts don't stretch, so the passengers can't move from their seats in a crash. ☐

Seat belts stretch slightly to increase the speed of the passengers compared to the car. This reduces the forces acting on the chest. ☐

Seat belts stretch slightly, increasing the time taken for the wearer to stop. This reduces the forces acting on the chest. ☐

Q2 Fay measures the activity of a sample of pure copper-64 in her home. The graph below shows her results.

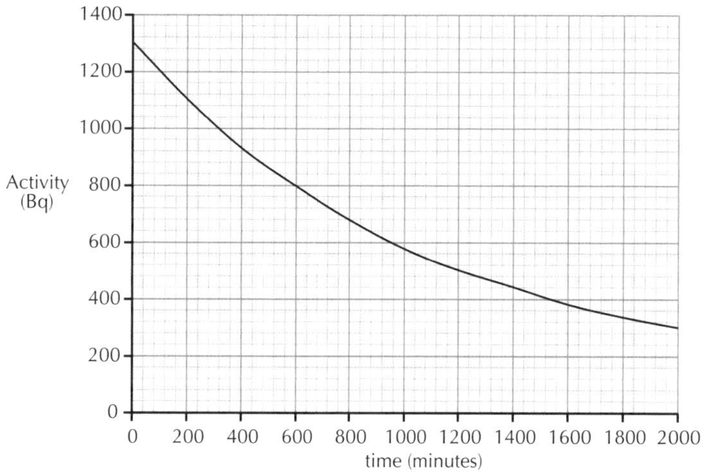

a) Fay had previously measured the background radiation to be **100 Bq**. Draw a line on the graph to show the activity of the sample **not** including the background radiation

b) Use the new graph to find the half-life of the sample.

....

....

....

c) Fay measures the background radiation at her friend's house and finds that it is much higher. Suggest **one** reason why the level of background radiation is higher there.

....

Mixed Questions — P2b Topics 4, 5 & 6

Q3 The diagram below shows part of a nuclear chain reaction.

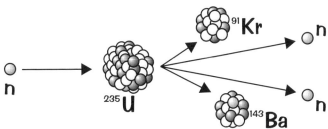

a) What is the name of the type of nuclear reaction shown in the diagram?
Tick the box next to the answer.

☐ nuclear fishing   ☐ nuclear fusion

☐ nuclear fission   ☐ nuclear fiscal

b) Describe what happens in this chain reaction.

....

....

....

c) Nuclear chain reactions need to be controlled.
Draw lines to match up each part of a control system with how it helps control the reaction.

moderator

absorbs neutrons so
that the chain reaction
can be slowed down

control rod

slows down the fast
moving neutrons

d) When this reaction is used in a nuclear power station it creates pollution.
What pollution does it create? Circle the answer.

carbon dioxide   radioactive waste   toxic gases

e) Give **two** ways that people who work with nuclear radiation can protect themselves.

1. ....

2. ....

<u>Mixed Questions — P2b Topics 4, 5 & 6</u>

Q4   Cobalt-60 is a **radioactive isotope**.

a)   Explain how the atomic structure of cobalt-60 ($^{60}_{27}$Co) is
different from the structure of 'normal' cobalt-59 ($^{59}_{27}$Co).

....

....

b)   What does it mean if a substance is radioactive? Circle the answer.

It decays (breaks down) into other substances and gives out radiation.

It emits radio waves.

It will only emit radiation when it is moved.

c)   Cobalt-60 gives off gamma rays.
Circle the right word to complete the sentences describing gamma rays.

> Gamma rays are **high** / **low** energy waves from the electromagnetic
>
> spectrum. They are **strongly** / **weakly** ionising and they penetrate
>
> a **long** / **short** way into materials.

Q5   Nick and Rob go on a roller coaster. With them in it,
the roller coaster carriage has a total mass of **1200 kg**.

$G.P.E. = m \times g \times h$

a)   At the start of the ride the carriage rises up to its highest point of **60 m** above the ground
and stops. Calculate its gain in gravitational potential energy. Use g = 10 N/kg.

....

....

....

b)   One of the carriages needs to be repaired. A super strong
handyman pushes it **120 m** from the ride to the repair workshop.

i)   Calculate the work done by the handyman,
if he pushes the carriage with a constant force of **85 N**.

$E = F \times d$

....

....

ii) Calculate the power output of the handyman if he pushes the carriage for **100 s**.

$P = E \div t$

....

SXFW44